MR
GIG

MR
GIG

NIGE
TASSELL

First published in 2013 by
Short Books
3A Exmouth House
Pine Street
EC1R 0JH

10 9 8 7 6 5 4 3 2 1

A CIP catalogue record for this book is available from the British Library.

ISBN 978-1-78072-161-3

Printed and bound in Great Britain by
CPI Group (UK) Ltd, Croydon, CR0 4YY

Cover design: nathanburtondesign.com

For Jane, Finn and Ned
  – always the headline act

Contents

FOREWORD

THE PUNTER
Prefab Sprout, Portsmouth Guildhall, 6 November 1985

The spotlight's beam cuts through the fug of smoke and dry ice. It picks out the singer, an unlikely pop idol with his DH Lawrence beard and Graham Greene-referencing songs. At his feet – front row, centre-stage, pole position – are five soft-faced teenagers gazing up at their deity of choice. Among them, the skinny literature student losing his live music cherry in this chintzy municipal hall of burgundy carpets and polite usherettes. It's not CBGB's. Nor is it The 100 Club. The band don't snarl or spit or scare or swear. But, as I decline illicit cigarettes and sip under-age pints, my skin is prickling just the same, aroused by the ceremony of live performance. I'm a convert. Afterwards, a sniff around the stage door to (unsuccessfully) touch the hem of the singer's garment, a bag of chips and a sprint for the last train. The snatched set-list gets Blu-Tacked to the bedroom wall, a souvenir of this new world, this promised land, this Narnia. And, lying back in bed, head spinning with lager and excitement, I vow to go back through the wardrobe again.

THE PROMOTER
The House Of Love, Essex University, Colchester, 2 June 1989

I'm lost in the shadows. Here in the wings, coils of cables at my feet and the stench of unwashed roadies in my nostrils, I can see everything. But no-one can see me. Several hundred expectant faces gaze up, oblivious that I control them. Simply pressing a few light switches makes them come alive, turning expectation into ecstasy. The object of their anticipation is The House Of Love, *the* indie outfit of the moment. They're at my shoulder, just as eager, just as expectant. My fingers hover over the light switches. I wait for the nod. The band wait for the nod. The sound guy gives that nod. I kill the house lights. Darkness. The crowd roars. The House Of Love stride forward. The crowd roars even louder. The Saturday night ritual none of us tire of.

THE REVIEWER
Terry Callier, Fleece & Firkin, Bristol, 10 February 1998

I need the loo, but there's no chance. It's rammed. No-one has more than a single square foot of floor space. Bodies are so tightly packed that I can't even get my notebook and pen out of my pocket. And I need them – tonight I'm taking my place among the assembled press corps.

Somewhere behind me is the man from *The Independent*; a few feet to my right are *Mixmag's* correspondent and photographer. Discomfort and full bladder aside, I can't deny I rather like this position – an ego-pleasing place on the guest-list and the knowledge that my thoughts on this evening's entertainment will be read by many, perhaps even agreed with by a few. I've arrived. I am now officially a Music Critic. And reviewing gigs soon becomes second nature, Terry Callier the first of many artists who find their careers completely unaffected by my words of either praise or derision.

THE SUPPORT ACT

Manu Chao, Fiddlers, Bristol, 16 February 2002

I'm standing at the back tonight, but not as the semi-detached, war-weary reviewer with one eye on a swift exit. Instead, in a role for which, curiously, I appear to be increasingly in demand, I'm the DJ charged with keeping the capacity crowd entertained before and after the main attraction. Participant, not observer. Manu Chao and his band are on the dancefloor right in front of me. It's nearly 2am and, having finished their sweaty marathon set, they still have sufficient energy left to throw some shapes to whatever tunes are chosen by me. High adventures on the wheels of steel? In reality, I'm standing behind a couple of temperamental CD players that are balanced precariously on a wobbly trestle table. No matter. For the next half-hour, or as long as the trestle table holds out, I'm king of the world.

THE RECLUSE

Christmas nativity play, Winscombe Woodborough Primary School, 15 December 2009

The view's pretty decent but, Christ, these must be the most uncomfortable seats in the history of live performance. But I suppose they are designed for six-year-olds, not for the widening backside of a forty-something biscuit enthusiast. And what can I compare them to, anyway? This is as close to a gig as I've been for many, many months. In fact, I can't remember the last time. The angels and shepherds shuffle on stage, accompanied by the inevitable collective "aaah" from the assembled mums and dads. I sip my tea, dunk my digestive and sneak a furtive glance at my watch. Should be out of here by half past and back home in time for tonight's episode of *Location, Location*. That's a wild late night these days. If my younger self – the fresh-faced gig debutant, the teenage promoter, the twenty-something reviewer or the DJ in his thirties – could see me now, he'd surely be appalled. How has it come to this?

1

WHERE DID OUR LOVE GO?

People used to call me Mr Gig. They don't any more.

Student entertainments officer. Roadie. DJ support act. Promoter. Gig reviewer. Punter. For much of my adult life, live music has been everything, nothing else getting a look-in. Where others' lives are defined by the performances of under-achieving football teams, mine is measured by gigs. Years are recalled not by births, deaths, marriages or relegation dogfights, but by other, equally crucial criteria – such as the size of the salsa orchestra David Byrne brought to Brixton Academy in 1992, or by how many times I could see Gorky's Zygotic Mynci in a single month in 1998 and still clock in at work at 9am the next day (I managed six).

First dates weren't ever conducted in the back row of the movies; they always took place in the front row of some gig, usually in a less-than-palatial dive in the arse-end of town. Deciding to visit friends at weekends was always determined by when a certain band was playing in the provincial outpost a particular pal was holed up in. And whenever love broke down, I always had the sympathetic shoulder of live music to cry on.

Whenever I bumped into someone I hadn't seen for a while, they wouldn't bother asking about my health, my family or my opinions on the government of the day. They'd cut to the chase. "So, what good gigs have you been to lately?" Live music was my identity, the context people unfailingly put me in. To them, I seemed to operate outside the normal parameters of everyday life, floating around in my own, loudly amplified universe.

I was an addict. I could go a maximum of four or five days between gigs without suffering from withdrawal. Usually it was much less. And it never mattered where the action was – the grotty upstairs room of a pub or the velveteen seats of a municipal concert hall, the sticky-floored students' union bar or the soggy lower paddock of a festival-hosting dairy farm. I wasn't fussy. I just couldn't stay away.

How did I get here? Slow off the mark when it came to meeting girls and learning to drive, but it was the opposite with music. First out of the blocks. Everyone else eating my cinders. When you grow up several miles past the back of beyond, in a coastal town they forgot to close down, you need *something*, after all. And I found music – or music found me – nice and early. By the second year of junior school, I knew the lyrics of each and every ELO song – and also had a little playground sideline in facsimile auto-graphs of the band's tightly permed leader, Jeff Lynne. At secondary school, I was never without an Our Price carrier bag in my clutches, the badge of adolescent musical obsession. A different day, a different LP. I spent seven long years borrowing and lending records with the few other kindred spirits in my class, those who also saw more worth in exchanging the Factory Records back catalogue than in swapping Figurine Panini football stickers.

But while the record collection grew and grew, I remained a stranger to live music until I went to university. We were barely on speaking terms. I'd love to regale you with romantic stories of bunking out of the bedroom window to go and see The Clash at the age of 12. But I can't. There aren't any. Nor can I tell tales of running off to fanatically trail Aztec Camera or Orange Juice around the country in my school uniform. Far from it.

For the unrepentant music addict I considered myself to be, the total number of gigs I went to before I left home for university was shameful. (Here I'm tallying up proper gigs. Not those featuring a shoddy, third-rate bunch of amateurs in a pub of a Tuesday night, but real concerts with tickets and roadies and lights and dry ice and support acts. And, in the better-heeled auditoria, the opportunity to buy ice cream in a tub at half-time.)

The number of these proper gigs wouldn't have troubled the digits of one hand. They won't trouble you for long, either. They were:

- Prefab Sprout, Portsmouth Guildhall, 6 November 1985
- U2, National Exhibition Centre, 4 August 1987
- REM/10,000 Maniacs, Hammersmith Odeon, 12 September 1987
- Mahlathini and the Mahotella Queens, Bishop Otter College, Chichester, 18 June 1988

Admittedly, it's not a bad first list to kick off with. Nothing too embarrassing there. No Shakin' Stevens, no Hot Chocolate, no Black Lace. Little reason to hang my head in shame at the quality. Just the quantity. Four. Quatre. Vier. Cuatro. Whatever language you say it in, it's pitiful.

Things changed overnight when I scraped together some half-decent A-level results and sloped off to university. My accommodation might have been on the 12th floor of a tower block served by a pair of temperamental lifts, but it was also a mere 150 yards from the main campus venue. No more post-gig sprints for the last train, no more carefully negotiated lifts home. No more excuses for not being there.

But I knew that the view from the front row wouldn't be enough. At that gig a few months earlier by the masters of South African township jive, Mahlathini and the Mahotella Queens, I'd been deeply impressed that it had been the college's students who'd organised it. Then I found out that one of my radio heroes, Andy Kershaw, had done exactly that job when he was at Leeds University. I fancied a slice of that action.

The moment I arrived on campus – before I'd even introduced myself to my new flatmates and bagged a spot in the communal kitchen cupboard for my pile of long-life Vesta curries – I signed up for the students' union Ents team. A freshers' week double-header featuring hairy Midlanders Pop Will Eat Itself and London rapper Derek B would be my backstage baptism. And from my first grunted exchange that afternoon with a real, live, builders-bum roadie, I was hooked. I worked each and every gig, usually in the service of a band I cared little for. My love was blind. Essay deadlines were missed, but I was always there right on the dot whenever a scruffy Transit van, filled with war-scarred instruments and equally battered amps, rolled up and needed unloading.

Within a few short months, I had stood for the post of Ents Officer and somehow got elected. And, with that 12-month apprenticeship served, live music defined me further in my post-university life: the cynical roadie, the fingernail-chewing independent promoter, the pre-show DJ and the gig-reviewing music journalist. And, mostly, the enthralled punter.

Why had live music taken such a grip on me? It's not as if, after the first dozen or so gigs, it holds too much mystery. You pretty much know how things will pan out: the polite, lukewarm reception for the support band; the headliner going on stage later than contractually agreed; the pantomime of the encore. But the ceremony of live music – however time-worn, repetitive and predictable – never lost its allure.

I've never kept a diary nor ferreted away a collection of ticket stubs, so the grand total remains uncalculated. But the number of bands I've seen must run into the thousands. Among them have been some exotic affairs, pilgrimages to the music bars of uptown New Orleans, the all-night clubs of West Africa and the accordion-filled streets of Mexican border towns. But most of the time – at least 99.7% if we're being scientific – it's been through the doors of various Guildhalls, Corn Exchanges, Bierkellers, Town & Countrys, Rock Citys, Purple Turtles… those cathedrals of live music cited in the sacred texts (the gig guides of the *NME* and *Melody Maker*), crucibles of worship for congregation after congregation of hopelessly devoted disciples. They were my spiritual homes too.

Were, were, were. As ABC's Martin Fry once declared (somewhat overdramatically, I always felt), that was then, but this is now. That was the old me and these are just memories, war stories, fireside tales. The adventures stopped happening. The front door stayed shut.

❧   ❧   ❧   ❧   ❧

It's a long time since the whiff of dry ice was in my nostrils, or since I woke up with mild tinnitus. Since I blagged my way onto guest-lists three or four times a week. Since I questioned exactly what services were covered by the indecent booking fee I'd just paid. I can't remember the last band I supported as a DJ, nor the last time my fingers reached to switch off the house lights to plunge a packed venue into darkness.

Those times are starting to feel as though they were all a lifetime away, dimming and dissolving like the memory of a past girlfriend. And my relationship with live music was like a love affair – a steady, reliable one that occasionally bordered on the obsessive. There was no ultimate showdown, no tumultuous break-up. Ours was a quiet, almost imperceptible parting. But, yes, other people were involved.

Two people, in fact – Finn and Ned. A pair of blond-haired lads, all smiles and Spider-Man fixations. And what fatherhood brought with it dwarfed whatever was lost when live music drifted off my to-do list. Gig-going was the first casualty. I became the de-mobbed soldier, the constable removed from frontline policing and into a desk job.

These new arrivals needed dedication, security and routine, not a commitment to parenting that wavered according to whoever was currently on tour. And they needed it most in the evenings and nights, usually right at the hour when the headline act would be taking to the stage. From now on, the only light show I'd witness would be when Finn was bouncing around his darkened bedroom with some glowsticks; the only time I'd hear "1–2, 1–2" was when little Ned was practising his counting.

Saturday nights now meant excursions to Asda, not the Astoria. Evenings became more PTA than NWA. And the only time that my DJ skills got called upon was when I was operating the volume control during Pass the Parcel at a kids' birthday party. Live music slipped away and, captivated by fatherhood, I really wasn't missing it. No more grunted discourse with monosyllabic roadies. No more employing a charm offensive to get into a gig when your name's been left off the guest-list (again). No more writing a live review in the darkness of a venue because your copy deadline is precisely 15 minutes after the head-liners leave the stage.

I was no longer in the thick of things. I wasn't even in the thin of things. I simply wasn't there.

Putting parenthood ahead of music can make for the odd uncomfortable moment. Last Saturday morning, Johnny Green – The Clash's legendary gonzo road manager during their most potent years, whom I recently interviewed – called me at home. With embarrassment and fumbling fingers, I made a dash to turn off the song on the kitchen stereo. It was not *Brand New Cadillac* by The Clash. It was *Big Red Car* by The Wiggles, the astonishingly annoying but phenomenally successful

Australian beat combo aimed squarely at the three-and-under market. (If you don't know of them, congratulations. Do your very best to keep it that way.)

Of course, a healthy proportion of almost any gig's audience will be made up of mums and, more likely, dads. Parenting and gig-going are far from mutually exclusive. But I was also now a victim of geography. A few years before Finn arrived, Jane and I had moved out of Bristol, our home for the previous half-decade, and into the Somerset countryside. The move gently applied the brakes on our social lives – the house required total renovation and a newly arrived collie-cross needed a lengthy romp across the fields every evening. It was a simple equation. DIY duties + post-dog-walking energy levels + a 50-mile round trip to see a gig of any credibility = a growing distance between live music and me.

And as much as I love the Mendip Hills – their rugged beauty, their innate spookiness – they can never be described as a hotbed of live music. Yes, some little bash called Glastonbury inhabits its eastern fringes for one weekend most summers, but day-to-day, week-to-week, month-to-month, it's a cultural desert for the gigging crowd. Unless – regional stereotype ahoy! – you fancy seeing The Wurzels in some remote haybarn where rosy-nosed locals dispense moonshine cider into whatever receptacle you've brought with you. (This is absolutely true. I have seen it decanted into one of those plastic petrol cans you keep in your car boot, then consumed through the screw-in nozzle. Perhaps the spirit of rock'n'roll isn't completely absent round our way after all.)

It might sound ridiculous that a man who derives all his income from writing about music – a music journalist to give the job its proper title – can be so disconnected from the live circuit. But I am. I do most of my interviews over the phone, an arrangement that suits me – a two-and-a-half-hour, £140+ peak-time train ride away from London – just fine. And when I'm not racking up a chunky phone bill trying to track down a recalcitrant musician in a hotel somewhere between Pittsburgh and Peterborough, I earn my money reviewing new releases, a duty that can be performed anywhere in the world with a reliable postal service and an internet connection. Even deepest Somerset.

That this is my trade is clear from the quickest glance at my working environment. It's no longer the cavernous venue waiting to be filled by the queue gathering outside. It's a cramped spare room that doubles up as a walk-in wardrobe. Promotional CDs are stacked on the desk eight piles high, battling it out for any available space with an untouched hillock of ironing. Even if I'd recaptured that urge to get out and go to gigs on a more regular basis, further towers of CDs – unrequested, unwanted and earmarked for the Oxfam shop – are blocking my path to the door.

And, were I able to squeeze out of the door, there are plenty of reasons why a gig wouldn't now be my first port of call. There are the astronomical ticket prices, for starters. The sea of mobile phones obscuring the view. The price of a room-temperature can of lager. The decision of bands from my youth to casually jettison any original artistic principles and reform for one big payday. The incessant chatter of those in the crowd who believe a gig is a social gathering and that the live band is a mere accompaniment to that. The renaming of once-iconic venues to include the monikers of mobile phone or drinks compa-nies. Having to stand in a muddy field several hundred yards away from the stage, only able to see your distant heroes on the big screen... I could go on.

In a few weeks' time, I'm going to be 41½. Yesterday, in one of the crusty magazines in my doctor's waiting room, I read that the current life expectancy of a UK male is 82.6 years. Not a bad innings by anyone's stand-ards, and a figure that will surely be nudged a little higher over the next few decades by medical advances and improved diets.

But as things presently stand – and as long as I'm both lucky and average – I've just edged over the halfway mark, the brow of the hill. And I don't want it to be all downhill from here, the years unravelling as modern life disappears both out of reach and out of sight, vanishing as quickly as my hair down the plughole of the shower every morning.

Since I left the doctor's surgery, all the clichés have shot to the forefront of my mind. Where's the time gone? What have I done with my life so far? And what needs to be done with the remainder? These are surely the early signs of a mid-life crisis. And it's a crisis I need to avert. I haven't got the cash to splash on a sports car or a high-per-formance motorbike. I've no desire to embark on a string of extramarital affairs. And I'm too much of a shit-scared wuss to take up anything that can be broadly defined as an 'adventure sport'.

This morning, the *Today* programme is all a-flutter with speculation about who's going to be announced as this year's Glastonbury headliners. A text arrives from my mobile phone provider offering me discounted tickets at any and all of the concert venues that now bear their name (which are many). I tip some cereal into my bowl. The packet boasts "a massive festival ticket giveaway".

Now I'm not a spiritual man. Nor am I superstitious. I think things just happen. This morning, though, it's different. Radio 4, the spam text message, the cereal packet – they're all clearly signs. A finger beckoning me towards the light. An invitation to return to the fold. Live music is calling me, I'm sure of it. She wants me back.

This is how I'll give that midlife crisis the slip, how I'll return to the world beyond the spare room and the school run. But it's not simply about trying to recapture my youth. It's about engaging with a changing world. After all, I don't want to be feeding solely on those old war stories for the rest of my life, to be that never-in-my-day reactionary in the corner. I've just got to make my peace with live music's 'evolution', its new ways.

I finish my cereal and, on the way back from dropping the kids off at school and nursery, take the long walk home. This is what I do when I'm having a think. Open fields, fresh air, clear brain. A plan is hatching.

Jane's in the kitchen when I get back. "Hon…"

I moot the idea of a multi-legged road trip where I bugger off to find out just what the hell live music's all about these days. I carefully reason that, now Ned's toilet-trained and Finn can amuse himself for hours on end with just a Roald Dahl audiobook and some drawing materials, they're not such a handful. A double dose of parental supervision isn't obligatory. And there's no dog that needs walking now that Jake the collie-cross has departed for the great ball-chase in the sky.

Jane seems very receptive to the idea. And why wouldn't she be? Not only is this a plan that gets that grumpy git out of the house, but her quiet evenings will no longer be punctuated by the snores of the uncivilised warthog that's passed out on the sofa. Maybe I'll even return home with a smile on my face. They don't see that very often round here.

I'm gratefully issued with a series of weekend passes, stamps of approval for me to temporarily divest myself of domestic responsibilities come Friday night and hit the highway. I pull the underused road map of the British Isles off the bookshelves, for the first time seeing glamour in the thick blue lines of our motorway network. I feverishly draw up an itinerary. It's one that'll take me far and wide, to some old haunts that need revisiting but mostly to places I've never been, home to musical experiences I've never had. Fuelled by festival falafel and overpriced service-station confectionery, my aim is to reconnect with live music, to fall back in love with its charms – at least before my ageing Honda Civic Estate uses up its ninth and final life on the snow-coated hard shoulder of the A1(M).

There are many questions to be answered: Am I looking to regain my youth? Can I make peace with middle age? Will I get my groove back? And, most crucially, is the mosh-pit an appropriate place for a tubby, bald man on the dark side of 40?

2

ME AND THE FARMER

Destination: Worthy Farm, Pilton, Somerset
Occasion: Glastonbury Festival
Miles travelled so far: 34
Gourmet pies consumed: 3
Punters spotted dressed as nuns: at least 7
Fake airliner crashes witnessed: 1
Practical jokes played on me by a National Treasure™: 1

I think I know where I am. It's 2am, my vision is blurred and I'm more than a little disoriented. But, staggering to the top of this hill in near-total darkness, the lights of an ad hoc building make a wonderful sight, a warm, well-lit bosom into which I shall imminently be welcomed.

For this set of conjoined marquees is the field hospital here at, to give it its full name, the Glastonbury Festival of Contemporary Performing Arts. Thursday night is becoming Friday morning, and, while tens of thousands of revellers down the hill are warming up nicely for the weekend, I need treatment. My ailment is not the result of chemical over-indulgence. Nor am I carrying a freak crowd-surfing injury. Instead – sigh – I've got a touch of conjunctivitis. Rock'n'roll.

A kindly doctor in plain clothes called Matt issues me with a bottle of eye drops and I wander off into the night, marvelling at the miracle of this field hospital. I've been to plenty of late-night A&E departments, usually with a fevered child in tow, but have never known one to diagnose and dispense so speedily. Truth be told though, were there no healthcare provision here on the festival site, I could always have popped home to see what appropriate medication was lurking at the back of our bathroom cabinet. Because my journey cannot, at this point, be remotely described as an 'odyssey'. The Honda hasn't even used a single gallon of fuel yet.

I've started on home turf. If I stand on a chair, I can see Glastonbury Tor from my bedroom window. Well, if a big hill wasn't in the way I could. If I get out of the house, climb that big hill and then stand on a chair, I can see Glastonbury Tor. Definitely. On a clear day, at least.

And my knowledge of the back lanes of Somerset has allowed me to bypass the traffic queues, speeding here in little over half an hour from front door to farm gate. I did actually consider leaving the tent at home and undertaking a commute for each day that I'm here, an arrangement with the in-built advantages of a full night's sleep in my own bed, a leisurely breakfast and my regular morning dose of CBeebies. But no. If I'm going to get anything out of this whole trip, I've got to throw myself in with both feet. So into the car boot went the tent, the walking boots and the multi-pack of Imodium. Fresh bedsheets, Jane's transcendental pancakes and *64 Zoo Lane* are all cast aside.

Earlier today, before the dust and the hayfever conspired to worsen the conjunctivitis, I sat on the steep slope near The Park Stage, on the site's most southerly reaches, and drank everything in. To my left, a man dressed as some kind of gold-laméd pirate was tumbling down the hill, locked in a friendly wrestling hold with another man kitted out as a Power Ranger. At the bottom, they narrowly avoided colliding with – and this will appeal to anyone familiar with the opening titles of *The Monkees* – someone decked out in Victorian nightwear who was being pushed around in a full-size, proper-job wrought-iron bed. Then, striding into my eye-line came a near-naked Catweazle lookalike, his diminutive leather loincloth successfully covering his meat but losing the battle to conceal his two veg. The surreal nature of this 20-second tableau is not atypical. This is Glastonbury. All human life is here.

And all is on a vast scale, covering far more of the local landscape than I remember. That's possibly because – and despite the proximity of Worthy Farm to our house – it's well over a decade since I was last here during festival time. Those were the years when huge numbers, certainly of Bristol's population, would descend on Pilton without a ticket and sneak their way in by way of a collapsed section of fencing or a leg-up from a kindly stranger. This was, of course, before the controversial 12-foot-high 'super-fence' was erected. It was also long before gourmet pies became readily available at outdoor music events. I was last here as long ago as 1997, the first year of the legendary mud baths, the opening salvos of the festival's ongoing trench warfare. I don't want to underplay in any way the terrible conditions and sights encountered by the legions of First World War soldiers at Passchendaele or Vimy Ridge or any other grim battle on the Western Front by comparing them to late-90s Glastonbury. Sure, there was no shellfire, nor grenades. But, to a cosseted soft-as-shite modern man, how more hellish can your existence get than if the zip on your tent refuses to move in either direction and your sole canister of Camping Gaz ran out on Friday evening?

General discomfort aside, musically 1997 to me meant a super-sharp Supergrass, an incendiary set from The Prodigy (all flashlights and booming bangs) and chuckling as The Levellers were pelted with clods of mud. The overwhelming consensus is that Glastonbury that year belonged to Radiohead, with a performance that's since been voted the greatest the festival has ever seen. I'm rarely around when history's being made; accordingly, I missed this defining set, otherwise engaged in trying to get across the site to catch David Byrne on the JazzWorld Stage, one gloopy step at a time.

The thigh-strengthening quagmire of 1997 is a world away this weekend. Traversing the site is still a test of stamina though, only this time the earth is scorched, not soaked. All paths between the main stages are powder-dry, throwing up puffs of dust with every step. My bloodshot eyes are not grateful for this. Remarkably, some of these puffs of dust are generated by a few pessimistic souls wearing wellies. Just in case. You never know.

But a sudden downpour really isn't going to happen. The skies are cloudless and shade is at a premium, even causing some to take refuge in the long shadows cast by the foul-smelling Portaloos. The last time I was so drippingly hot at a festival was at the Chelmsford leg of V96. The temperatures were pushing 80 degrees and the open parkland site boasted one single, solitary tree offering shelter from the sun's unrelenting rays. Any forays to the mosh-pit that day were interspersed with lie-downs in the shade beneath the Super Furry Animals' decommissioned tank.

The weather isn't the only difference between my last and my current Glastonbury experiences. Tickets in 1997 cost £75. They're now £185. If this near-300% price hike were made by a utility company or privatised train operator in such a comparatively short space of time, it would keep the tutting classes, swallowing whatever editorial bile the *Daily Mail* aimed in their general direction, apoplectic for months. But Glastonbury has a glut of goodwill among the gig-going nation. It isn't a faceless corporation. In fact, it's got a very human face – one that, rocking the beard-but-no-moustache look, is instantly recognisable across the land. And across lands beyond our own, it seems, as shown by *Time* magazine's anointment of Farmer Eavis as one of the 100 people "who most affect our world".

He's done a sterling PR job of reversing the opinion of the nation. Nowadays, several of those previously tutting newspaper editors never fail, come Glastonbury weekend, to run a front-page photo of some easy-on-the-eye gap-year student enjoying the delights of Worthy Farm, whether launched onto her boyfriend's shoulders in bright sunshine or wearing an ad hoc raincoat fashioned from a couple of bin-liners. As if to demonstrate just how far the good farmer's bash has ascended in the eyes of the establishment, yesterday, while his mother made a visit to the tennis at Wimbledon, Prince Charles dropped by Worthy Farm to make an appearance on the Pyramid Stage.

Not only was 1997 the last year I was here, it was also the first year that the BBC televised the event. Maybe it's been the mud that's scared me off in the years since. Maybe the event's growing acceptance by Middle England has kept me at arm's length, even though I live just up the road. Almost certainly, the Beeb transmitting the circus straight to my living room, where a range of light refreshments are to hand and where a dry 4-tog duvet ensures a full night's sleep, has proved too alluring. I'm not alone. In the years ever since, the BBC's broadcasts have been how the mud-phobic majority have experienced the Worthy Farm carnival.

I'm keen to see how the corporation distils the essence of Glastonbury and sends it into the living rooms of the nation. I've popped backstage behind the Pyramid Stage and am waiting for Caroline, 6Music's press officer, to give me a guided tour of the BBC compound. While I wait, one of the tankers that collects and removes the contents of the latrines is going about its business. The air is ripe with the eye-piercing stench of ammonia and human faeces. Everyone covers their noses and turns away. It's not all glamour behind the velvet rope, you know.

My first impression of the compound, once the tanker's departed and Caroline's flashed her pass to the security guard manning the five-bar gate, is that it resembles the lorry park of a motorway service station. There are huge trucks everywhere, mainly those familiar battleship-grey vehicles of the BBC Outside Broadcasts department that you see outside the grounds of your favourite football team – if, laments this Colchester United fan, your football team is good enough to ever make an appearance on *Match of the Day*.

Inside the 6Music production office, the station's newshounds Julie Cullen and Matt Everitt are busy compiling reports from around the site. Further along the desk, presenter Gideon Coe is studiously preparing to be next on air, presumably researching probing questions to ask his imminent guest Jack White. It's certainly not just a case of turn up with a few microphones, have a wander around the site and transmit the results. If planning the festival itself is a head-spinning masterclass in logistics, coordinating the broadcast output also requires an unfathomable level of organisation.

Attached to the outside wall of the 6Music studio next door is a series of print-outs, the size of which make them more bedsheet than spreadsheet. These detail all the interviews and live recordings due to be broadcast over the next 24 hours. They are to-the-minute precise. It's hard to imagine the Normandy Landings being planned in tighter detail. A quick glance tells me that singer-songwriter Kate Nash is the next artist due to climb the steps into the tiny, windowless mobile studio, the interior of which is no bigger than the average semi's box room. I spin round and see that she's right behind me, bang on time for a light grilling from Lauren Laverne, the presenter currently on air. (A bit later on, I experience the full rush of a fanboy meeting one of his idols when I spy the still-very-cool Johnny Marr waiting to go into the studio.)

While the interviews go out live, the performances don't. Across from the 6Music studio is the imposing truck of the BBC's Compliance Unit, a department more crucial than ever in these times when the corporation is being shot at from all directions. The unit's job is to listen to and/or watch all the performances before they're deemed suitable for transmission. It's a good job, too. Snoop Dogg's polite requests to "put your motherfucking hands in the air" might not appeal to the less enlightened members of the teatime BBC audience who've tuned in for *Songs of Praise*.

It's not just the presence of royalty in both locations that prompts comparisons between Glastonbury and Wimbledon. There are similarities geographically – the Pyramid Stage is Worthy Farm's Centre Court, the Other Stage is Number 1 Court, and those innumerable, far-lying stages the more minor outside courts. There are also parallels in their respective television programmes. Both are still slightly haunted by the voices of broadcasting titans past – Dan "Oooh I say!" Maskell in the case of the tennis, John Peel for Glastonbury. Furthermore, Lauren Laverne is in effect the Sue Barker of the Beeb's Glasto coverage – the player who, on hanging up her guitar/racket, turned presenter. Barker's best Wimbledon as a player was when she reached the semi-finals of the Women's Singles in 1977, agonisingly close to the ultimate prize. Lauren's best Glastonbury as a performer was probably in 1998 when her welly-booted band Kenickie played the Other Stage, just a single step removed from a spot on the Pyramid Stage.

Lauren's a busy bee come Glastonbury weekend, seemingly never off either 6Music or BBC Two. Having watched proceedings from the comfort of my sofa for more than a decade, I want to ask her whether she feels what the corporation beams onto the nation's plasma screens and through its DAB radios is a fair reflection of what's actually happening on site. After all, my fellow TV viewers could sometimes be forgiven for thinking the action only takes place on the three largest stages and in the BBC's backstage compound.

"There's no perfect way of doing it," she later tells me. "You can only really be subjective. The bands on the John Peel Stage or up at The Park tend to be my kind of thing, but that's not the same for the other people on the team. So between us we get quite a good mix. But you can't get it perfectly right. If you go to Glastonbury and you have an itinerary and you have to hit everything on time, you're missing part of the experience of just letting things happen. I think you have to have a similar attitude to the coverage. Capturing the spirit is what's important, rather than the actual timeline."

Lauren's fellow TV presenter Mark Radcliffe has, since Peel's death, increasingly found himself cast as the great man's replacement, the wise elder around the backstage campfire – "or the grumpy old bastard for which I'm eminently well qualified!" he suggests. I'm wondering to what extent, given the logistical and scheduling invest-ments the BBC has made in the festival, the presenters need to keep smiling, need to keep that balloon in the air. After all, on their rota of presenters, there is no stern Alan Hansen figure analysing the performances and saying what, on occasion, might need to be said.

"We've had a sort of situation like that with Willie Nelson," Mark confides. "Now, I love Willie Nelson. He's a legend and he's written some amazing songs. He's definitely someone who should be on. He was, however, bloody awful! So you're put in a difficult position. I won't exactly say 'This was kamikaze defending', but you do try to have a certain kind of honesty. Not everybody is fantastic and some value judgements are made. If someone was down for having three or four songs televised but they were duff, they might be cut down to one. The viewer could make a critical judgement on who's good and who's bad by seeing who's on the telly and who's not. But then you get someone like Leonard Cohen who unfortunately didn't want to be filmed at all, so we couldn't put any of that out when he was absolutely wonderful."

When he's not being disappointed by a Willie Nelson performance, Mark does get plenty of time to wander the site and imbibe the whole shebang. "It's a complete spectacle. I haven't been to every festival in the world, but I've not seen anything like it. I've been to Reading and found it pretty grim. The marvellous thing about Glastonbury is the effort that's put into things that just look nice – things that are just memorable and atmospheric on the eye, but don't actually do anything. It's the utter pointlessness of a lot of it that makes it rather wonderful. The fact that people would take half a helicopter, paint it pink, weld it to half a stuffed elephant and cart it across the country to the site seems rather marvellous to me…"

※ ※ ※ ※ ※

I remember when all this was open fields.

Allow me to rewind a few months. It's the previous April and I've been sent on assignment down here to Worthy Farm, not for an achingly hip music publication but for cuddly old *Countryfile* magazine. My brief is a tête-a-tête with Britain's most famous farmer – Athelstan Joseph Michael Eavis.

I have to admit that, as tête-a-têtes go, this is no classic. A rigorous cross-examination, with all the intensity of Frost taking on Nixon, it certainly can't claim to be. The interview is being conducted in Michael's Land Rover as we rumble around the empty fields. But the combination of its noisy engine and Michael's willingness to pull over every 30 yards to chat with the workers preparing the site isn't lending itself to particularly high-level discourse flowing back and forth.

I can forgive him for being distracted – he's got rather weightier matters on his mind than responding to my questions, many of which he's probably answered scores of times before. Indeed, when I first rolled up to the farm, I got the feeling he thought *Countryfile* the TV programme was visiting. "You're not the normal chap," he said with a hearty handshake. No, I am not John Craven.

And despite the demands on his time, Michael remains remarkably grounded, never one to toot too loudly on his own trumpet. He might be the avuncular steward of one of the most remarkable live music events ever created, but he seems to prefer talking about the day-to-day activities of the farm. Rather than indulge himself by recalling a string of celeb-filled anecdotes, he concentrates on the more prosaic chapters of his life story. "I milked for 40 years non-stop," he proudly reports, "from when I was 19 until I was 59. Hardly ever had a day off. 40 years!" Tales of Springsteen and Bowie and McCartney remain under wraps; instead I get a demonstration of the electrical device constantly circling the cattle shed and sweeping all the cow shit off the floor. We stand admiring the technology, before the nearest animal to me lifts its tail and evacuates its bowels, splattering my boots and prompting the good farmer to unleash his tremendous laugh.

Now we're back in the Land Rover, bumping and scraping along the muddy tracks and across the empty fields that, within three months, will be completely transformed. Only the skeleton of the Pyramid Stage gives a clue about the double life of this otherwise unremarkable dairy farm. By now, *Countryfile*'s photographer has nabbed the passenger seat to get some shots of Michael behind the wheel, leaving me to ride al fresco in the back. As this means I'd have to continue the interview by poking my dictaphone through the rear sliding window and asking questions using a hefty amount of sign language, I abandon the cross-examination and settle back to enjoy the bone-shaking ride. My enjoyment is short-lived. Very quickly I realise that the Land Rover is heading straight for a large, presumably deep puddle, one at least 15 foot wide. Has he not seen it? He's certainly making no attempt to drive around it. Time to take cover. The Land Rover crashes through the puddle, sending a large plume of muddy water over the cab and into the open rear section. I quickly assume the foetal position to avoid a soaking. Michael looks over his shoulder through the sliding window, his guffaws roaring across the valley.

Although keen to play the playful practical joker and at ease with being regarded as a Great British eccentric, Michael is also fired by both a steely professionalism and an unstinting sense of social justice. The price of admission to Glastonbury may have risen sharply in recent times, but the proceeds go to good causes. The coffers of CND, Greenpeace, Oxfam and Water Aid have all been swelled by festival cash over the years, while the village of Pilton's infrastructure has also been greatly improved, with the festival underwriting the building of social housing, along with a regenerated village hall and brand-new post office. This all helps Michael to find peace with his neighbours after decades of local opposition. This year is the first that the festival's licence was granted without a single letter of complaint. You must be doing something right, Michael. "Yeah, after 40 years!"

No-one can argue that there's little disruption to Pilton's everyday ways. The festival does ask its neighbours to show a great deal of tolerance and understanding as its staggering logistics disrupt their quiet lives. Here are a few numbers to mess with your mind:

- 2,000,000 litres of water are used every day during the festival
- There are 4,600 toilets on site, including 670 metres of urinals
- Nearly 2,000 tonnes of waste are generated over the weekend, half of which is recycled
- 40km of fencing has been erected to protect the farm's streams and rivers from becoming contaminated
- The ad hoc car parks accommodate an estimated 45,000 vehicles
- Shuttle buses make 4,000 journeys between the site and the nearest mainline railway station at Castle Cary.

With figures like these, you can understand why the residents of this normally sleepy village might get a little concerned about their quality of life being compromised come late June. Opposition would certainly be more militant were the proceeds disappearing into personal bank accounts, but the greater good seems to be the priority for Michael. "We're not going round in a shiny new Range Rover or anything. I'm just happy with this one," he announces, patting the steering wheel of our current battle-worn chariot. "My wife's got a Mini. That's plenty good enough. We don't swank. I'm not pleading poverty or anything, but we just don't go overboard. My actual wage for the festival is less than I pay my cow man. That's not so bad, is it?"

As we head back up the hill towards the farmhouse, Michael pulls the Land Rover over one last time and cuts the engine. He leans in closer, conspiratorially. "I don't really know why it works, to be honest with you. I really don't. It's like when you write a song and people like it – you don't know why they like it." More guffaws. I don't believe the canny old devil for a second.

Now coming back here in late June, aside from the low ridge of hills framing the site, the farm at festival time is unrecognisable from those empty April fields. I've spent most of Friday trying to get my bearings and have managed to return to my favourite vantage point, the hill near The Park Stage. There may well be plenty of colourful characters around that my inner anthropologist fancies observing, like yesterday's pirates and Power Rangers, but right now a plate of carb-heavy pasta is demanding my attention.

And I need these carbs to take me long into the night. The festival site measures one-and-a-half miles across, while its circumference is more than five times that. That's a lot of distance to cover. And I intend to cover it. I've set myself a challenge to visit as many of the 60 official stages (plus a handful of unofficial ones) in the next 36 hours as I can. I'm going to immerse myself in all the festival has to offer, a bulimic gig binge after years of fasting. I'll be zigzagging across the site, ticking each stage off, like a trainspotter collecting numbers at Crewe Station or a hillwalker edging closer to conquering all 282 peaks in the Munro list of Scottish mountains over 3,000 feet high. For every British Rail Class 67 locomotive or Cairngorm summit, I've got the John Peel Stage or Cubehenge or The Bimble Inn or The Rabbit Hole. Although I have to admit to being a little nervous about the delights offered by the stage known as Pussy Parlore.

I've opted for stages, rather than bands. In times past – in the less muddy years, at least – I would have tried to see as many bands as possible, adding new names to that lengthy list in my head of Bands That I Have Seen Live. (Here, a note of etiquette: in order to rightfully say you have seen a band live, at the very least you must witness two full songs, from intro to applause. That's the minimum requirement and them's the rules. Admittedly, they're my rules, but they're incontrovertible rules nonetheless.)

Even if I only caught two songs of every band I saw, I still couldn't hope to witness even a tenth of this weekend's performers. And there will always be a multitude of conflicting acts fighting for your attention. Half an hour ago, for instance – and depending on which direction I'd taken – the soundtrack to choosing my dinner could have been provided by Vampire Weekend on the Pyramid Stage, Florence & The Machine on the Other Stage, Mumford & Sons in the Peel-saluting stripy marquee, Plan B on the East Dance stage or Reverend And The Makers in Leftfield. And those are just the bigger stages. I could also have unwittingly stumbled on the delights of Horse Meat Disco in the Dance Village.

Yes, frankly, there's too much here. It's dizzying and dazzling. For now, I'm content with watching the current turn on The Park Stage down the hill in front of me. They're a couple of scruffy blokes – one on acoustic guitar, the other on piano – who seem to have drawn an impressive-sized crowd. They now appear to be playing Radiohead's *Karma Police*. But who are they? Surely Farmer Eavis hasn't rubber-stamped the booking of a Radiohead tribute act. I check my pocket guide. 'The Park. 8.30. Special guests.' The penny drops. It's an unannounced perform-ance from Thom Yorke and Jonny Greenwood, two-fifths of Radiohead. I might have missed them in 1997, but have inadvertently caught up with them well over a decade later. Some neat, if unplanned, circularity.

As an orange-red sun slips behind the hazy blue hills to the west, the congregation are in fine voice, assisting Yorke on the haunting refrain "I lost myself...". This is undeniably one of those Glastonbury Moments™. The fact that the pasta's hitting the spot, and the eye drops are working, only adds to the sense of both occasion and well-being. God bless you, Dr Matt.

I think I might lose myself tonight. Geographically, I mean, rather than spiritually or pharmaceutically. I still haven't completely got my bearings and the encroaching darkness isn't about to improve that situation. So, using the southern boundary of the super-fence as my reference point, I head due east. I know it's due east because it's in the opposite direction from that setting sun. Ray Mears, me.

Having passed through the Tipi Field, I soon reach the Stone Circle in King's Meadow, the highest point on the farm. These standing stones have been arranged to mirror the Cygnus star constellation, but its builders didn't need to gaze up to the skies for inspiration. They should have just looked down at the site from this vantage point. The darkening fields are now linked by necklaces of twinkling lights, a sight as beautiful as any distant constellation.

Striding purposefully through The Healing Field, specifically along the ad hoc thoroughfare known as Soothsayers' Avenue, around me all manner of treatments are peddled and predictions made. But I'm not particularly in the mood to have my runes read or my aura recalibrated. I'm too busy checking my messages to see what kind of day Jane and the boys have had back home on Planet Earth.

"Cast down your phone!" booms a voice. I look up. It belongs to a tall, topless white guy of indeterminate age. He could be anywhere between his late twenties and early forties. Certainly those mangy dreads will have taken a good few years to look as lived-in as they do.

"Welcome to the true festival. No phones allowed! You have left Babylon now." His outstretched arm directs my gaze back down the hill, to the sea of light and sound. To Babylon.

There's no hint of irony; his lips aren't shaping into a knowing smile. In fact, it's only his references to my phone that tell me he's addressing me – his eyes seem to be gazing into the middle distance. Judging from his detached demeanour, I suspect his career trajectory to not be that stratospheric. Perhaps he's a poet who does a little light gardening on the side. Or maybe he advertises his services with a card in the newsagent's window – Personal Shaman For Hire. Or, more cynically, perhaps he's able to indulge in this lifestyle because it's underwritten by a buoyant trust fund. He might now answer to a Mother

Earth-saluting name like Sunrise or Thunder, but I suspect his mother still calls him Rupert.

Although I'm keen to point out to Rupert that some of the immodest prices being charged along Soothsayers' Avenue suggest Babylon's tentacles have actually reached The Healing Field, he has got a point. Things up here are a little calmer and considered, closer to the spirit of the first festival in 1970. I can understand how the belch of competing PA systems and bare-nosed commerce down in the valley would make you beat a hasty retreat, to head for the hills.

Plenty of souls have beaten such a retreat. Many of them are dressed in a way that you would never choose to if you were popping out for a pint of milk. Who are they? Where do they come from? And what do they do when they're not utilising the Vale of Avalon's ley-lines to channel higher forces? I suspect they're the folks so vividly portrayed in the Half Man Half Biscuit song *24-Hour Garage People*, the "weekend pagans" who "probably work in an all-night garage, with Talk Radio on...".

If they do work in service stations or local government offices or sell insurance door to door, who am I to denounce their off-duty personas? If they're incarcerated in a call centre for the other 51 weeks of the year, repeating their phone scripts over and over again, why shouldn't they be allowed to go wild in the country? This is a right granted by most festivals, and by Glastonbury in particular: the right for people to be extroverts, to reinvent themselves for three or four days away from the 9-to-5 grind. "It's an escape," Mark Radcliffe reasoned. "The normal rules of society cease to apply. You check in on Thursday night and leave the world behind until you get out again. That seems to me to be a seductive notion, that you're visiting an alien land."

For now, I need to leave the alien lands of The Healing Field and head back to Babylon. Gorillaz are on the Pyramid Stage at ten o'clock and it's going to take me a good half-hour to get across there. Longer, in fact, if I stop off for pudding on the way, which of course I do. I place my order at a stall run by a bunch of good-looking long-haired types of both genders – lots of piercings, plentiful sun-and-stars tattoos. Their smiles seem genuine and welcoming but, like the futurologists and homeopathy practitioners up in The Healing Field, these young hippies certainly know their free-market economics. I pay £4.50 for a very modest cup of tea and a minuscule chocolate brownie barely bigger than a postage stamp. It's the size of a Penny Black – and near enough the price of one too. And although on the mend, my sticky, half-open conjunctivitis-ridden eyes can't tell the difference between the salt and sugar dispensers. Into the tea goes a healthy shower of salt. And into the bin goes the most expensive un-drunk cuppa in all Christendom.

Featuring cameos from a multitude of guest artists, Gorillaz offer better value for money. Their set, as close to an old-fashioned revue show as anything else this weekend, encapsulates the myriad sounds of Glastonbury, stitching together classical Chinese and Indian musicians, De La Soul, heavy dub bass, legendary soul crooners, hip-hop beats and two members of The Clash (dressed, for reasons lost on me, as sea captains). Damon Albarn is clearly something of a silver-tongued devil when it comes to persuading some of rock's grouchiest individuals to take part; Lou Reed, Mark E Smith and Shaun Ryder are all up on stage joining the jamboree. With such a multinational cast, the one-world spirit of '70 is, for an hour or so, available down here in the depths of Babylon. Someone should tell Rupert.

As each legend is welcomed on stage, several thousand camera phones are raised to immortalise the moment, both blocking my view and causing me to sigh. I woefully ponder, not for the first time, how if you're capturing the experience of watching a band by taking a few dozen photos or shooting some video, you're going to be seeing a large part of the gig through your phone's screen. The taking of the photos or video becomes what you actually experience. My theory about the practice's ubiquity centres on the rise of digital music. Without a physical object to touch/gaze at/keep on a shelf, consumption of recorded music becomes invisible. So the capturing of *live* music, an in-the-moment experience previously only recalled after the event either through memory or a bootleg cassette, compensates for this loss. A few ill-focused pictures or some wobbly footage becomes what's lacking elsewhere, something physical, tangible. A souvenir. Theory aside, what's definitely happening is that my view is being diced by the multiple arms raised aloft as camera phones are held up in the air.

Although I find it easy to resist capturing the show in this way, I am enjoying it, particularly the game of guessing which notable person is going to be wheeled out next. But, while Sister Sledge once claimed to be lost in music, I'm not in such an altered state. That's because I'm paying so much attention to staying on my feet. Here on the right-hand side of the mammoth crowd, it's a seething scrum – I've been lifted completely off the ground three or four times. I haven't felt this tightly packed in since the days of oversubscribed football terraces in the mid-'80s and I need to get out. It takes a full 20 minutes to emerge from the pack, a task made all the more difficult by a man resolutely riding his bike right through the middle of the sardine crowd. Somewhat unreasonably, he's impatiently ringing his bell when the crowd doesn't – *can't* – part to allow him through to carry on whatever business needs his attention so urgently. Perhaps his chakras have become so dangerously misaligned that he frantically requires emergency treatment up in The Healing Field.

My feet might now be on solid ground, but the view's not great from here and I end up watching the crowd rather than the show. According to *The Guardian*'s review that runs the following day, the punters on the other side of the audience are similarly distracted: "A large portion of the crowd on the left of the field spends five minutes watching a man atop a wooden pergola, exposing first his arse and then his penis before descending amid a hail of bottles, a spectacle with which the electro-soul elegance of *Empire Ants* just cannot compete."

As a cloud of Chinese lanterns rises into the sky to join the yellowing full moon, I take my leave from the Pyramid Stage and get on with the task of visiting as many stages as possible. At first, I try to make this a journey without maps, to allow my instincts to take me wherever they wish to go. It's only when I pass the Croissant Neuf stage for the third time in 20 minutes that I swallow my pride and take out my map, with only torchlight to guide me. The well-meaning folkies playing this particular marquee ("powered by the sun!" it proudly proclaims) aren't enough to snag me. I'm after something more epic and I'm heading to the site's most south-easterly fringes to find it.

Arcadia is my first stop, a post-midnight extravaganza featuring pumping techno and drum & bass, fireballs, vast lasers, trapeze artists and a gigantic spider under which a range of dance music acts perform. Arcadia is the kind of spectacle you'd expect to accompany a Jean Michel Jarre arena performance or to be set up on London's South Bank for New Year's Eve. Instead, the mammoth set has been painstakingly erected in a dusty cow field in deepest Somerset, and that's hard not to admire.

From Arcadia, I head across the old railway line to Shangri-La, an area that I'm even more taken with. This is the festival's most outlying suburb, with an identity very much apart – a mysterious, post-apocalyptic netherworld of art installations and entertainment. Now that the main stages have shut down for the night, this is many people's after-hours destination of choice – part futuristic city-scape, part film set, part sin-soaked souk. It's a dystopian graphic novel come to life.

Artists, set designers, builders and carpenters have taken weeks to construct it, and the effort that's been invested is extraordinary. My eyes are agog at one partic-ular sight. The front fuselage of an airliner has been set up to appear as though it's crashed onto the festival, the ground around it dug out and the branches of nearby trees deliberately dislodged as though the plane has come to a dramatic, premature end on its descent into Bristol Airport. The only unrealistic element is the full-on rave that's carrying on inside the hollowed-out fuselage.

I spend a good ten minutes marvelling at this creation, before heading off along a key part of Shangri-La. The

Alleys are a warren of vice and iniquity. Imagine *Blade Runner* or *Mad Max* set in the narrow passageways of Marrakech – passageways, that is, that have been decorated by street artists – and you're about a quarter of the way there. As I stumble through these corridors of alternating darkness and bright light, I decide not to give my business to one of the local hostelries, a cabaret bar called Fish & Tits that offers "live music and dangerous women". Elsewhere in Shangri-La, the "no tattoo, no entry" policy of The Snake Pit disqualifies me from passing over its threshold, something of a shame as I quite fancied the invitation to "live out your last days watching dark toxic cabaret". I consider scrawling on my skin with a biro to gain entry, but instead plump for catching an ace ska band at the Deluxe Diner, the perfect early-hours soundtrack to this most exuberant of Glastonbury's outlying suburbs.

Leaving Shangri-La at sometime around 3am, I take about an hour to wander back to my tent on the very far side of the site. I'm serenaded at various points by booming drum & bass, moonlit folk sessions, a horn-heavy gypsy band playing as they march along, and some performance poetry that really is unnecessarily shouty at this time of night. By the time I reach my tent, my feet are sore and I'm more than a bit niffy, but I'm buzzing. Sleep won't come soon.

After three hours of fitful kip on an inflatable mattress that stubbornly refuses to inflate, the heat arrives early the next morning. My eyes are now fully functioning, though, so I'm ready and willing to return to the fray. At the stall run by friends of mine who sell silver jewellery from the Sahara, I ease myself in with the twin pleasures of shade and mint tea. The latter does wonders in desert conditions, after all. Realising I haven't squandered all my money on miniature chocolate brownies, I buy Jane a Tamashek necklace as thanks for putting up with a weekend's worth of young boys' temper tantrums while I'm having a high old time a few miles away. Guilt assuaged, it's off to catch a lorry-load of music, following an itinerary that pinballs between stages. I know Lauren Laverne guarded against such prescribed behaviour, but in forgetful middle age, I really appreciate a to-do list. And among those ticked off are Devendra Banhart, Beach House, Jerry Dammers' extraordinary Spatial AKA Orchestra, Field Music, Midlake and my old pal Seasick Steve who, three years on from holding court with me in the back of his campervan, is now entertaining tens of thousands up on the Pyramid Stage. Absent from the list are my fellow Somersetians The Wurzels. I can do without a crowd of ironic London types taking the piss out of us locals.

A few performers get missed. Not only do the stage times of Candi Staton and Kelis clash with each other, but more importantly they clash with one of my meal breaks. Both singers lose out to the delights of Bristolian pastry merchants Pie Minister where I plump for the tried and tested Heidi – goat's cheese, sweet potato, spinach and red onion. Even when faced with an endless selection of gastronomic delights from all four corners of the globe, when I'm hungry I'm something of a flat-earth thinker, an unadventurous soul. It's my third pie of the weekend.

Scheduling clashes abound all weekend, throwing up some impossible conundrums. Pet Shop Boys or George Clinton? Northumbrian folk sisters The Unthanks or *I'm Sorry I Haven't A Clue* legend Jeremy Hardy? The Phenomenal Handclap Band or a debate about the banking crisis?

By 6am on Sunday morning – and after another cross-site sortie to gaze in wonder at the delights of Shangri-La – I strike camp, make a half-arsed attempt to squeeze the folded-up tent into its canvas bag and head for the car park. I've had an invigorating, enlightening time, even if I didn't manage to find all the stages I was hoping to. (It wasn't until a few days later that I discovered that the location of the elusive Rabbit Hole is a tightly held secret and accessed only by both answering a Lewis Carroll-related riddle and scrambling on your hands and knees along a narrow, dark tunnel.)

Thanks to that recalcitrant airbed, I'm a little bruised, not to mention somewhat malodorous, but at least this time, unlike 1997, I'm not returning home with mild trench foot. The lanes are quiet and I'm back in time for breakfast. More importantly, I'm back in time to take Son Number One to a birthday party. I suspect it won't stand up to comparison with where I've just been, no matter how many Quavers and Chipsticks they're serving.

While a pack of five-year-olds go absolutely mental on the bouncy castle (two nosebleeds and counting), I nurse a plastic cup of weak orange squash and reflect on the last few days down on the farm. Once the conjunctivitis eased, I had a blast. Yes, it's far more corporate than the days of yore, but it avoids becoming a larger version of every other festival thanks to those numerous pockets of independence and invention scattered across the site. And it's an undeniably safer and more sanitised place these days. Maybe it's my age, but I kind of agree with Mark Radcliffe when he says that he has "no great nostalgia for the days when the fence was kicked down and thousands of people just piled in". Those could be miserable times.

Now, pretty much the only frowns I saw all weekend, away from those belonging to injury-nursing casualties in the field hospital at least, were on the faces of those lining up at the massive Orange tent to get their phones charged who had just realised how long and slow the queue was.

If you turn a blind eye to the many instances of rampant commercialism (one of the general stores charged me a quid for a single Bic biro when mine ran out), the original hippy ideals of love, peace and harmony are far closer to hand now than they were during the years when opportunistic, fence-scaling scallies rampaged their way across the camping fields, looting tents for whatever valuables they could pocket. I've certainly enjoyed going about my day on Worthy Farm without the worry, experienced during previous eras, of returning to my tent to find myself relieved of my worldly possessions (which, back then, admittedly only amounted to an unreliable Walkman and a couple of faded REM T-shirts).

For punter and performer alike, Glastonbury's 21st-century incarnation seems to suit all. This weekend will be the high-water mark for many bands, the point at which their careers will rise no higher. They know this is the pinnacle, that it's now a graceful, hopefully slow descent to whence they came. They've performed at the world's greatest festival, after all – the musical equivalent of having had a trial for Manchester United. The story is safe and stored, to be dusted off for the grandkids' pleasure in 30 or 40 years' time. "Did I ever tell you about the day I played Glastonbury…?"

But not all bands go gracefully into the night. Some don't make peace with the dimming of the day, with whom they once were and with whom they are now. Like many of us, they're still out there trying to recapture their youth, anxious to turn back the tide of mortality. And that's where I'm going next.

3

BEST DAYS OF
OUR LIVES

Destination: Temple Island Meadows, Henley-on-Thames
Occasion: Rewind '80s Festival
Miles travelled so far: 256
Performances by former *Smash Hits* cover stars: 10
Boy George lookalikes spotted: 7
Number of times asked for own autograph: 2

"Apparently the announcer's gone for a shit, so I'll announce myself. I'm Carol Deckerrrrrr!"

I wasn't aware that a Honda Civic Estate possessed the power of time travel. But, like Michael J Fox at the wheel of his DeLorean, I've clearly just driven through some strange portal, skipped back three decades and been deposited slap-bang in times past – in our case, the 1980s. In whichever direction I look, there are signifiers: big hair, shoulder pads, day-glo garments. And the collective memory of the decade being of a brash, unsubtle period in popular culture is born out by the potty-mouthed introduction that T'Pau's flame-haired singer has just given herself.

This is the Rewind Festival, a two-day celebration of '80s pop, a salute to the hit-makers of yesteryear, coaxed out of retirement by the lure of a not-ungenerous pay cheque and the renewed adoration of a five-figure audience.

I'm of the right age to belong here. But I don't.

I've driven to this sunny riverside meadow in Henley-on-Thames with a heavy heart. Two reasons. One is that I'm not exactly comfortable with groups reforming and re-emerging into sunlight after locking themselves away in dusty retirement for a decade or two. Why are they happy to exhume their younger selves, to reheat those past glories? You had your time. Now move on. Do something else.

The other reason for my Eeyore mood is that affairs like Rewind are responsible for condensing the '80s into a crass caricature. Just as Spangles and space-hoppers became shorthand for the '70s, the ten years that followed have been compounded into a crudely drawn, garishly coloured cliché. Rewind is a festival that represents what the '80s now mean to most, the time when taste and understatement apparently took a decade-long holiday. There's more day-glo on display here on a single afternoon than I clapped eyes on in the entire decade. Even more than you'd see at a national convention of car-park attendants.

Then there are the jumpsuits, headbands, ironic mullets and suit jackets with the sleeves rolled up to the elbow *Miami Vice*-style. Some have gone further. Like the four guys over there in full *Ghostbusters* regalia. There are also several men of a certain age – and a certain unfavourable body mass index – who've turned up independently as *Do You Really Want To Hurt Me*-era Boy George, all dreadlocked wigs and heavily applied eyeliner. Later I watch a woman, dressed faithfully as Adam Ant's dandy highwayman, good-naturedly remonstrate with a security guard who's denying her access to the backstage area. Getting no joy, she then pulls out a replica flintlock pistol to persuade him a little more...

I'm not at all concerned that I'm underdressed, sporting neither eyeliner nor packing a flintlock. I don't go a bundle on the notion of grown-ups wearing fancy dress. What right-thinking adult does? But – if it were a mandatory requirement of entry today (which most seem to think it is) – I'd have plumped for a donkey jacket with a CND badge or two on the lapel, a Coal Not Dole T-shirt, black Levis with turn-ups and a pair of utilitarian DMs. I might even be whistling The Specials' dystopian classic *Ghost Town*.

Because Rewind isn't *my* experience of the '80s. This is the version that only existed in the pages of *Smash Hits* or inside the *Top of the Pops* studio. But it's the version that endures in the collective memory. All those inconvenient, complex events that pockmark our life and times have been jettisoned. Nostalgia is a business that trades on happy days and collective repressed memory syndrome. When it comes to the '80s, there's no room for recollections of war, famine, economic uncertainty, strikes, civil unrest and the very real threat of nuclear Armageddon. As they didn't wear luminous fingerless gloves and weren't proficient behind a synthesiser, striking miners and warring world leaders have been airbrushed out of the picture.

But I don't want my dark mood to simmer any longer. For the time being, I leave matters of historical accuracy well alone. The sun is shining, after all, and it is lunchtime.

I join the queue at the falafel stand and am instantly cast into shade by the towering chap in front in full Robocop costume. Drifting across from the main stage comes the unmistakable parping trumpet from Modern Romance's *Ay Ay Ay Ay Moosey*. I'm trying my best to stay positive. Honestly, I am. But this song is undeniably one of the decade's musical low points – and there were more than a few. Have I really driven all this way for this? Right now I could be stretched out in the back garden, a G&T within arm's reach and my ears filled with the more pleasant sound of Finn and Ned bouncing in and out of their paddling pool, giggling the afternoon away.

I find a spare patch of grass and concern myself with the most pressing issue of the hour – the grasp of engineering required to keep falafel, hummus, salad and tahini sauce within the confines of a single pitta. This was a talent I nurtured at festival sites across the country. I'm delighted to find that it's a trick this old dog can still do. My shirt stays clean.

But can the old dogs up on stage remember what to do? Modern Romance are the first of today's dozen acts, each of whom will deliver a fun-sized, attention-keeping set of around 25 minutes. My ears soon tell me that some might struggle with even this modest a time-slot. Modern Romance weren't the decade's most prolific hit-makers and, to fill their allotted time with crowd-pleasing tunes, are now resorting to an extended version of Chic's *Boogie Wonderland*. Later on, Imagination – still fronted by the excessively vowelled Leee John – will turn a similar trick, dropping into their set both a cover of sunshine soca fave *Hot Hot Hot* and a medley of Bob Marley tunes. I can feel those dark thoughts returning.

But, while certain acts lack the back catalogue to do it justice, this short-set format works really well. Lukewarm about one particular hit-maker? No problem. Simply trot over to the food concessions for a quick refuelling and another will be along in a few minutes. And it's the hits all the way.

The pace is relentless, an eight-hour juggernaut of music with between-set DJs keeping the momentum high. They play almost every big, bright anthem of the decade. (Although, somewhat curiously, they seem to have neglected to bring along copies of either Bauhaus's *Bela Lugosi's Dead* or the Dead Kennedys' *Too Drunk To Fuck*. Schoolboy error there, chaps.)

As the Thames gently flows on past, there are no moments of peace or quiet reflection here on the river-bank. Glastonbury's Healing Field seems a world away. Over to my right, a pair of young girls, ten or eleven of age, are singing – well, shouting – their hearts out to every tune the DJs are spinning. Neither girl would have been born until at least the tail end of the '90s, but both are word-perfect. They're currently trying to hit the high notes on Europe's *The Final Countdown*.

I blame the girls' mum. Debra, a teaching assistant from High Wycombe, has not only brought along her daughters, she's also insisted on decking them out in that obligatory day-glo. One girl's got canary-yellow leg-warmers. The other is wearing what appears to be a homemade bright pink snood, the woollen hood-cum-scarf creation made infamous by diminutive popster Nik Kershaw and recently revived by a number of lily-livered, ooh-it's-a-bit-chilly Premiership footballers.

I can't let this go without passing comment. "This is the music of my youth," defends Debra, with little hint of apology in her voice, "and I've been playing it ever since. I'm afraid it's all the girls hear around the house." Poor things. Should I consider calling the authorities? Debra laughs, somewhat falsely, clearly out of politeness. "I suppose it's a little cruel imposing my music on them, but all these songs bring back such strong memories. Boyfriends, school days, your first kiss… I can't resist it."

My heart sinks. But what about discovering *new* music? Are you really going to be listening to these old tunes when you're in the retirement home? "I've gone the best part of 30 years hearing these songs over and over. I can't see it stopping now. They'll never wear out." That's more than a bit depressing. It's one thing to stick with the music you know. It's quite another making it the soundtrack of your kids' lives too. Wang Chung's *Everybody Have Fun Tonight* now fills the air. Its key lyrics are "Everybody have fun tonight/Everybody Wang Chung tonight". I leave Debra and the girls to it, and go looking for more positive signs. These are scarce on the ground.

Towards the beer tent, I can see a couple of stag parties in competing states of advanced refreshment. The party to the left, dressed to a man in bedsheet togas, appears to be winning. A hen party approaches. Led by the bride-to-be, identified by those de rigueur L-plates, the hens are every bit as oblivious to the onstage action as the stags, whose undivided attention they now have.

I stick out like a sore thumb, the snooty, amateur anthropologist taking notes while all manner of human behaviour erupts around him. I'm a sitting target. A conga line of overly gregarious folk jinks its way in my direction.

Fancy dress is one thing. A conga line is quite another. And a conga line of people in fancy dress is worst of all.

I know these people. You do too. They live in your town. They're the people who, when in plain clothes and not a-conga-ing, treat gigs as social gatherings where they can noisily update everyone on their personal lives in mind-numbing minutiae. Meanwhile, a softly spoken singer-songwriter struggles to be heard up on stage. You tell them to be quiet. They ignore you. You hate them. So do I.

I nip to the left to evade the lurching conga line, but the leader is equally nimble, forcing his disciples into a sharp right turn. Shit. There are too many picnics sprawled across the ground to get away. He calls to me. "Come on, join us!" I refuse to meet his gaze. A gaze that will undeniably be the gaze of a cult-leading mass murderer. I look at his T-shirt instead. It says 'William The Conga-er'. Ye gods. No spontaneous demonstration of the conga dancer's art, this. He's *planned* these hi-jinks.

I consider pulling out my National Union of Journalists card and brandishing it like an officer of the NYPD would his badge, before making a citizen's arrest for crimes against puns. And, on behalf of my comrades in the Musicians' Union, crimes against live music. But it would be me versus the 20,000 and I don't fancy an early death. Suffocation by snood. Beaten unconscious with an espadrille.

Still refusing to make eye contact with William lest he hypnotise me into involuntarily joining his merry cult, I bravely mutter an inaudible "Erm, no thanks" and shuffle off towards the stage. Even seeing a wonky performance by those lightweight pop-funkers Imagination beats William's idea of fun.

Maybe it's me, not them. Twenty thousand people can't be wrong, can they?

To try to get more into the spirit of the occasion, I buy a mint-choc Cornetto, that most popular ice cream of the '80s, and wander towards Rewind's backstage area. I know how much the increasingly well-lubricated punters are enjoying themselves, but I want to find out how the performers feel. Pride or embarrassment? Dignity intact or slight distress that their entire lifetime is defined by a few moments in the sun the best part of 30 years ago?

First, though, I need to make my way through this gaggle of autograph-hunters who've paid extra to get into the VIP area. A rather staggering £100 extra, in fact. For that expense, they're still not close enough to invade the artists' personal space, but they are one set of panel fencing closer to their heroes.

Two or three autograph-hunters definitely have something of Alan Partridge's super-fan about them. They spend all afternoon and all evening on the same patch of ground, unable – and, bearing in mind that additional outlay, strangely unwilling – to actually see the performances. But they're in pole position to get an indistinct squiggle in an autograph album. It's unclear, though, whether these autograph collections will become treasured family heirlooms to be passed down to subsequent generations or be callously offered for sale on the internet by the morning.

Their modus operandi is the impolite cat-call. And they're pretty successful at getting what they want. Faced with the kind of adulation absent from their lives for the past 20 years or so, most performers lap it up, cheerfully wandering over to sign autographs over the fence. The more anonymous members of Kajagoogoo seem to be very much enjoying a long-missed ego massage. Anyone wearing a laminate around their neck is approached, book and pen thrust under their nose. Even me. The hunters' eyes are full of hope that I might be someone who made a significant contribution to the story of '80s pop culture. "Could you…?"

Should I try to pass myself off as someone else? Maybe the keyboard player in Johnny Hates Jazz or second trombonist in Dexys Midnight Runners? These are autographs that are bound to provoke a bidding frenzy on eBay, surely. And why stop there? Perhaps I could take it further, becoming a de facto member of Curiosity Killed the Cat by sneaking up on stage to thump a random piece of percussion during *Down To Earth*. But no. Bravery escapes me once more and I shuffle off to the Portaloo.

(Still, these requests for an autograph greatly amuse the troops when I get home. In a BBC poll, John Peel was once named as the 43rd greatest Briton who ever lived. His response was pure Peel: "I'm not even in the top five in this house!" Round ours, I share a similar standing, losing my place in the top four when the kids got a rabbit.)

Beyond the next section of fencing, a dozen or so Winnebagos are parked in two neat lines. The dressing rooms. Back here, no-one shares the concerns I'm loading myself down with. The performers appear completely at ease with the whole concept of revival shows. Middle-age contentment is the order of the day. But this raises further suspicions in me. Like a greasy tabloid hack snooping through the dustbins of the rich and famous, I edge shiftily around the backstage area, sniffing around for signs of bitching, of petulance, of long-held antagonisms that have simmered all these years.

I find none.

My concerns start to weaken. Those negative, dark-hearted preconceptions I drove here with are getting lighter. I can't be a misery all day long. While I see much of the shenanigans front of house as wholly inappropriate behaviour, I can't deny that everyone's just so normal and nice backstage. Once there might have been rivalry and petty jealousies, whispers and moans behind the scenes at *Top of the Pops*. Now it's all handshakes, hugs and comparisons of expanding waists and receding hairlines. Husbands and wives are introduced, shared histories are remembered. It all has the feel of a school reunion a full quarter of a century on.

And the performers seem to fully understand that what's occurring front of house is merely a version of the '80s; that – and this is something that very much pleases me – the day's bill of fare is far from the last word on the decade's music. I knock on the door of Heaven 17's Winnebago where Martyn Ware, one half of the now two-man group, is keen to pass on his perspective.

"I don't see the '80s as cheesy," he protests. "This facile view that they were all about padded shoulders and frilly shirts is nonsense. That's just convenient shorthand." The organisers have put jars of vintage sweets in each of the Winnebagos. Martyn offers me one. I really fancy a rhubarb and custard but my teeth aren't what they were when I was a ten-year-old rhubarb-and-custard addict. I don't want to lose a filling. Martyn opts for a Black Jack, finishing his point through a tough-chewing mouthful of licorice.

"You could easily do 20 different festivals based around different aspects of music from the '80s. Easily." He's not wrong. Despite the evidence to the contrary this afternoon, the music back then wasn't one long party soundtrack, all chirpy synths and big-haired choruses. It can't be reduced to this single definition, this one snapshot.

This was the decade when The Jam were the only band whose singles consistently went to number one on the first week of release, songs that railed against government defence spending or documented the shifting and increasingly grim lifestyles of a recession-hit population. This was the decade when The Smiths scored 15 Top 30 hits, outgunning more quintessentially '80s acts like Go West four times over. And this was the decade when the likes of ABC, Bananarama, Ultravox and Toyah all failed to land a number one single, a feat achieved by a quartet of spotty, devoutly socialist oiks from Hull called The Housemartins.

It wasn't just the variety of the charts. Martyn remains a fervent cheerleader for the quality of British pop music in those times. "I just downloaded this iPhone app the other day where you can dial in any date from the start of the pop charts and it shows you the Top 40 singles and albums." His flow is interrupted by the group's backing singer slipping past to use the Winnebago's loo.

"Just for a laugh, I went back to my birthday in 1983 when we were number two in the charts. From the Top 40 on that day, I can distinctly remember about 25 songs and they're still being played now. I honestly don't think that will be the case in 25 years' time with today's music. I think you'll be lucky to remember five songs." The blinkered view of a 54-year-old man trapped in the amber of his twenty-something life? Possibly. But it sounds pretty plausible to this 41-year-old trapped in a similar situation.

It's certainly a different world now. The landscape has radically changed since the brash old days of '80s pop. Back then, the seven-inch single and the LP, the latter now available on this apparently exciting (and unbreakable!) new format called compact disc, jointly ruled the waves. Recorded music was everything.

In the pop world, a 'live' performance was much more likely to be a lip-synching affair on a kids' show like *Cheggers Plays Pop* or *Hold Tight!* than it was about getting them rocking in the aisles at Hammersmith Odeon. Their audience was largely watching while lounging on their sofas, observing from a distance. Live shows – especially the month-long, zigzagging tour itineraries of rock'n'roll legend – were the preserve of rock bands. The pop stars stayed at home and made records.

And why not? The cotton was very high in the record industry. Sales were enormous. In the mid-'80s, it was possible to release a near-million-selling single in the UK and still not reach the number one spot. It happened to Ray Parker Jr in 1984 when his *Ghostbusters* theme tune stalled at number two on the chart, despite shifting precisely 974,001 copies. That's the equivalent of every citizen of Birmingham buying a copy.

Almost exactly 20 years later, incontrovertible proof arose that the backside had well and truly dropped out of the singles market. The week in October 2004 that Eric Prydz's *Call On Me* stumbled to the top of the charts, it was bought by a measly 23,519 people. That's the population of Melksham in Wiltshire, or Rawtenstall in Lancashire. These are small towns. And that's a small number of records.

So, as these shiny black discs of polyvinyl chloride headed for the museum shelves, artists increasingly focused on live music for their coin. The record industry ship was listing badly. The concert venue was the life-raft, offering safe passage to less choppy waters. March 2009 marked a watershed in this reversal of fortune, as announced by Will Page, chief economist at PRS for Music, the body that collects songwriters' royalties from record sales and live performances. His calculator was clearly still steaming from some heavy arithmetic. "We've been doing some maths back at the office," he declared on 6Music. "The changing of the guard has already taken place for the first time in the history of the British music industry."

The result of his calculations was stark. In 2008, the total revenue for the UK record industry was £896m. But the income for the live music sector – a combination of ticket sales and corporate sponsorship – had made the tills ring to the tune of £904m. This was now where the money was. And the divide between the two has been getting wider ever since. Previously, bands toured from the top to the tail of the land to promote and flog their new record. Now, increasingly, the role of a new release – whether physical or digital – seems to be to indicate that a bunch of live dates are imminent.

All hail the live show. All hail the festival. Ridiculously popular and undeniably bountiful.

This is why almost all of this collection of forty- and fifty-somethings before me haven't set foot in a recording studio for years. Even if the artistic inclination were there, the financial return would be a pale imitation of what it could have been in sunnier times. That's all perfectly logical. But there's one thing I can't quite wrap my head around. How can a band that has always cared about its art (Heaven 17 took their name from a pop group in *A Clockwork Orange*, after all) be willing to regurgitate the generation-old hits for a crowd largely in fancy dress?

"It's surprisingly easy," declares singer Glenn Gregory, now the recipient of an all-over number-one buzz-cut where that trademark cream-coloured, slicked-back mane once prospered. "We enjoy doing these things. They're good fun. But we also work with new artists. If people are willing to accept it, there isn't really a contradiction. It fits comfortably with who we are."

So, no moral quandary for Martyn and Glenn. I place myself in their shoes. Were I a hit-maker from times past who'd been offered the opportunity to taste again the surely addictive rush of many thousand bellows of approval, would I turn down the cash offer and draw a line under my past life, never to return? My snootier, more idealistic side would rip up the cheque there and then, preferring my 'art' to remain unsullied by mere economics. But snootiness and idealism don't come into things. These are pop stars. Their situation isn't the same as that of Johnny Rotten – a man who, let's not forget, previously wanted to "destroy passers-by" – reinventing himself as a butter salesman on TV. Pop music has always been about fun. It's not about light and shade. It's all about light.

Surely today's performers don't need the money. We know the clichés. Seeing out your days rattling around a stately pile somewhere, never having to do a stroke of work again. Filling that round-the-clock leisure time by tinkering around with quad bikes and trout farms.

After all, a writing credit on *Careless Whisper* alone has kept Wham!'s Andrew Ridgeley in surfboards and golf clubs ever since. And a quick glance at the cars in the artists' parking area shows that, unlike me, the star turns sure as hell didn't arrive here today in a crumpled Honda Civic Estate whose best days were around 120,000 miles ago.

I lean against a fence to make some notes. A guy, probably on the cusp of 60, approaches. He still has an enviably full head of hair and is wearing a comfortably expensive sweater, along with a tan that suggests he's no stranger to the golf courses of the Algarve. I'm guessing he's some music industry elder, a senior executive at some big record company. I don't know because I don't ask him. I'm trying to concentrate on scribbling down my latest pearl of wisdom before it leaves my brain. But he clearly wants someone to chat to for the five minutes it's going to take him to smoke his Marlboro Light. So, reluctantly, I do the small-talk thing. And I'm glad I do. He passes on a quite astounding revelation.

It's a revelation that will probably astound you, too. It's this: Heaven 17 only paid off the recording costs of their second album *The Luxury Gap* in the mid-2000s.

This is *The Luxury Gap* that was recorded in 1982. This is *The Luxury Gap* whose sales were certified platinum in the UK within a year of its release. This is *The Luxury Gap* that contained two Top 5 hits in this country, as well as another single that topped the Billboard Dance Chart in the US. In short, *The Luxury Gap* was, by even the most pessimistic definition, a successful record.

Maybe, after all, those big hits didn't set everyone up for life. Maybe today's performers are here out of necessity.

Maybe these appearances aren't simply about an ego boost or about having fun. Maybe the savings accounts are running dry. Is everyone looking back in hunger?

My informant stubs out his cigarette and wanders off, possibly to scramble someone else's head with another nugget of '80s pop trivia. I pull out my phone and call Jim Irvin. These days, Jim is both a music journalist and a songwriter for hire, performing the latter role for the likes of Lana Del Rey and David Guetta. But in the '80s he was the singer of the band Furniture. It wouldn't be incorrect to describe Furniture as a one-hit wonder, even if that sole hit – *Brilliant Mind* – is still much cherished by many today.

I need to speak to Jim. I need to find out what kind of royalties this afternoon's performers might still be receiving more than two decades on. Because, frankly, I have neither the tact nor the balls to ask anyone here to their face about the state of their finances.

Jim's at home and cuts straight to the chase. "*Brilliant Mind* was a moderate hit in one territory a quarter of a century ago," he reasons. "I have 40% of it. I'm not retiring on that." He casts an eye over his latest statement from the Performing Rights Society that details the song's recent airplay. It appears that BBC Radio Scotland is still particularly keen on it.

Every time a song is played on the radio in the UK, fees are paid twice over. One payment to PRS for Music, which collects on behalf of songwriters; the other to PPL, which collects on behalf of the musicians who played on that recording (whether band member or session player), a sliver of cash being split between all of those appearing. If it's a hit single, this can add up to nice sums during the weeks that the song is in the charts. Payments obviously drop off sharply when the single slips off the radio playlists.

A song's earning potential can return if someone else covers it and takes it back into the charts. But, as they didn't play on this new version, the original performers won't see a penny this time around. However, the writer or writers of the song will see their cashflow greatly improved. They get paid every time the song is broadcast, regardless of whose version it is.

So if you wrote 100% of a song that scored phenomenal success – maybe you were Troggs frontman Reg Presley and you wrote *Love Is All Around*, never off the airwaves in 1994 when Wet Wet Wet took it to the top of the UK charts for a tiresome 15 weeks – you could expect to live very comfortably for the rest of your days. (In Reg Presley's case, you could also expect it to fund extensive research into crop-circles and paranormal activity.)

The royalties earned through *sales* of the album or single – known as the mechanical rights – tell a sadder story. Even for a modest hit, these can be pitiful. Often they're non-existent. Royalties only kick in after all the recording, manufacturing and promotional costs have been covered. Though he continues to make money from *Brilliant Mind* as one of its composers, Jim has never seen any royalties from sales of Furniture's records. And this arrangement explains why Heaven 17 took so long to clear their debt. A new album simply brings new costs to add to the pile.

Even if these costs do get recouped (and record companies are notoriously creative when it comes to totting up the outgoings), royalties still represent a slender percentage of a record's retail price. And once the band's manager has taken his cut and the remainder is split across the group, at best there are just a few royalty pennies going into each member's pocket for every copy sold over the shop counter. And, of course, a few pennies are scant recompense. You might have put in a career-best performance on that record. You might have changed someone's life with the emotional way you played. But loose change would be your reward. The trout farm remains a pipe dream.

The best that an '80s pop star could hope for from a modestly successful career might be to live mortgage-free – as long as they bought their home when the cashflow was good and property prices were low. Early retirement was unlikely, even for a performer who'd enjoyed a chart-topping hit and perhaps a couple of other Top 10 singles.

"You probably couldn't live for the rest of your life off the winnings from one hit you recorded in your twenties," Jim reasons. "You might make the down payment on a house. You might even have bought it outright back then. But if you want to send your kids to college in the future, you probably need to get out there and earn a bit more in whatever way you can." And that's where plenty of this afternoon's performers come in.

Carol Decker seems to fit this profile. T'Pau did indeed score a chart-topping hit and a couple of other Top 10 singles. But she's resigned to her current place on the musical food chain, a good few rungs south of where she and the band were when swanning around in the very highest reaches of the US Billboard Hot 100. Now, heading back to her Winnebago after her set, she confirms that the revival circuit is something of a lifeline.

"I did attempt a solo career," she smiles, her post-performance glow not affecting her candour, "but no-one was interested. I put a single out on my own label but no radio station would playlist it. Yet the moment I step on stage to sing *China In Your Hand*, 20,000 people will be in front of me. I just have to accept that I've got other ideas that clearly no-one gives a shit about! But what am I going to do otherwise? Go and work in a post office or something?"

The relief in her voice is tangible; she is consoled by the existence of this nostalgia circuit that keeps her from a life of selling stamps and counting out pension money. "But if you'd told me ten years ago that I'd be singing to people dressed up as Ghostbusters, I'd be really fucked off! But if that's the way they see it, then that's fine. And I'm not exactly Lou Reed."

She leans forward conspiratorially. "But you will write that I was looking gorgeous and on-trend, won't you? Not dressed like a lunatic in leg-warmers..."

The woman who follows Carol Decker on stage – Altered Images' Clare Grogan – isn't dressed like a lunatic in leg-warmers either. For the purpose of performing just four songs, she's made some serious effort. Blue wraparound evening dress, gold strappy heels, diamante earrings grazing her shoulders. It's still only the afternoon.

But by her second number, Clare's experiencing something of a wardrobe malfunction. A more-than-gentle breeze has now gathered, blowing that wraparound dress skywards. "This is called *See Those Eyes*," she announces, pushing the dress back down. "Hopefully that's all you'll see." By the end of the song, Clare suggests she rename it *See Those Thighs*.

Her four songs quickly over, she's giddy and gabbling as she heads back into the wings. "There's a tidal wave of emotion happening to you, revisiting your youth like this. Holding it together is really hard. The memories madly rush back at you. But in a way it's not about the past any more. I know it's nostalgia but everyone who's here today is here to enjoy *this* moment." Maybe that's what I should be doing; enjoying *this* moment rather than putting everything in the context of the past.

We chat about how comfortable everyone is about peeling back the years to offer up, for public consumption, an updated version of the way they were. "None of us are under any illusions about what's happening here today. We're all grown-ups now. Back then, none of us spoke to each other. Not out of arrogance or being cool – we were all just teenagers and didn't have any social graces. We didn't know what to say to each other. Now everyone's quite sussed about it. In this environment, you'd feel quite stupid being the one who's having the strop about going on first. Actually, a lot of us are fine about going on earlier so we can get back to our children!"

How people make peace with life's relentless march forward fascinates me. I'm here precisely because I've yet to work it out myself. I could certainly learn a thing or two from Clare and her contemporaries. Like me, they too have crossed life's halfway point, gone over that brow of the hill. They don't seem bothered, though. Midlife crisis? What midlife crisis? "Back then I hated the responsibility of making everyone have a really good time," she confides. "I was so young. It absolutely overwhelmed me. Now I'm totally over that. I'm up there flashing my knickers. It doesn't matter any more. It doesn't matter *at all*."

I still have nagging concerns that I can't shift. If the future is supposed to be unwritten, why aren't today's performers keen to fill in the blanks? To be fair, some of them gave the whole revivalist concept deep consideration before signing up. Clare initially resisted the revival circuit's overtures, only giving in when her friend Kim Wilde told her how much of a blast these shows were to play.

The same was true of Level 42's Mark King. He's the latest performer to cross my path backstage. He too had serious reservations. This is the band's first appearance at Rewind. "I can't say that I was ever that keen to jump in and become part of a bandwagon," he explains, unable to restrain an ear-to-ear beam. "But that was fantastic. Absolutely brilliant."

He then says something that puts me right at ease. "There's something completely awesome about having the legs of your flares shaking from the breeze of a band in full flight stood up there in front of you. You can't cheat that. You've got to be stood there either in some hall or out in a field and letting it blast into you. Fantastic. You don't get any of that from a download or a ringtone."

At flipping last! For all the conga lines and stag parties, for all the Robocops and Ghostbusters, the essence of live music has actually made an appearance. That sense of direct connection to the music – not the frippery surrounding it – is what originally made me fall in love with live music. Whether the band are performing old hits or freshly minted new material is of secondary concern. It's primarily about the connection.

Indeed, like everyone on stage today, Mark doesn't unduly worry about the demand from punters to just hear the old hits. "I can completely understand it. If I were to go and see my heroes – I'm a big fan of Roxy Music's first album from 1972, for example – I would want to hear the stuff that meant something to me. I wouldn't mind if they wanted to play one or two new songs to see where they're going, but I'm not really fussed with what Bryan Ferry thinks he's coming up with now. What I really want to hear from them is the stuff that did it for me when I was 18, 19 years old, when it was fresh out of the box."

So it's effectively one big victory parade, a lap of honour? A grin and an enthusiastic nod. "Why not? We put the time in."

⁂ ⁂ ⁂ ⁂ ⁂

Having been persuaded that I shouldn't be over-thinking this whole nostalgia tilt, I head back out into the arena for a beer, the price of which is sadly the day's only concession to the 21st century. The stag parties are still in full cry as the cavalcade hurtles on towards sundown and beyond, foot still firmly on the gas.

Despite dressing like a pair of undertakers, Heaven 17 put in a never-too-cool-for-school set, complete with knowingly corny stage banter ("Who wants to come live with me? This is called *Come Live With Me*"). Jimmy Somerville, looking barely any older than when we first heard that impossibly high falsetto, goes down an absolute storm, reminding everyone of just how many hits he scored with Bronski Beat and The Communards.

Then I witness the day's most extraordinary performance. It comes from Rick Astley.

I remember Rick Astley as the shy boy-next-door type plucked from the obscurity of driving a van for his market-gardener dad to become the most valuable product of the Stock, Aitken and Waterman hit factory. Since then, he seems to have undergone something of a transformation. He now takes on the role of a leering holiday-camp comic. "Do you want it?" he bellows, rubbing his hands down his thighs in the manner of Vic Reeves on *Shooting Stars*, "'Cos I'm going to give it to you!" He apologises for a pre-set caffeine overload. "Ladies! Jiggle something for me. I've got to drive back down the M4 later. Give me something to think about!"

On a day when no-one's been remotely precious about their music, Astley takes it further by actually sending up his body of work. He slips into his biggest hit, *Never Gonna Give You Up*. "We've known each other," he soulfully croons, before yelling, "SINCE 1987!"

Looking across the crowd with just Boy George left to go on, I can't help thinking that Astley must have been delighted with his position on the bill. Ernie Wise used to say that, during their music-hall days, he and Eric Morecambe always preferred not to headline; that "second tops are better". This acknowledged both the weight of expectation on the headliner's shoulders and the fact that a clock-watching audience has its eye on the last tram home (which, here in our Thames-side location, translates as the last water-bus back across the river to Henley town centre). Boy George thus suffers. His is a flat, pedestrian set that never puts pedal anywhere close to the metal. Excuses are made, exits located.

I presumed I was going to put pedal to metal much earlier today. I've hung around a hell of a lot longer than I thought I would. To be honest, I surprised myself by even making it to the end of that opening Modern Romance set. But my feet are itchy now.

I shuffle towards the car park, resisting another visit to the falafel stall en route, and mull over the last few hours. Yes, it's been cheesy and unsubtle, and I'd normally run a mile from anything so high camp or purely pantomime. But, for a field full of punters baking their bonces under a burning sun, it's been unmitigated, harmless fun. In an industry defined by hyperbole, cynicism and mistrust, I'm deeply impressed by this uncomplicated innocence.

Rewind has not been the chronically dispiriting occasion I was dreading ten-odd hours ago. Indeed, today the bleeding obvious has dawned on me with all the impact of an anvil crashing down on Wile E Coyote's skull: that there is absolutely nothing wrong whatsoever with bands playing abbreviated, hits-only sets. It's what punters want and it's what the big festival stages must serve up to satisfy both existing fans and floating voters. The three-hour, obscurities-only, fanatics-pleasing live sets can be reserved for dark winter nights at the ICA or the Royal Festival Hall. Otherwise, let's keep things both familiar and brief. Be honest, now. Rare are the gigs where you don't get itchy feet after about an hour. You know I'm right.

I get into the Honda and ease back up the hill towards Henley town centre, passing through that time/space portal on the way. Back to the future. Tomorrow, the '80s become a memory again. The Robocop and Ghostbusters costumes will lie discarded; the highwayman outfit returned to the fancy-dress hire shop. And, for those performers enticed back into the sunlight for one August weekend, civvy street beckons.

As Clare Grogan's parting words had it: "I've had my J-Lo moment now. It's back to Budgens to do the shop tomorrow."

4

THERE IS A LIGHT THAT NEVER GOES OUT

Destinations: London, Liverpool, Bristol, Cardiff
Occasions: Reunions with Pixies, The Wedding Present, Big
    Audio Dynamite, The Smiths (sort of...)
Miles travelled so far: 1,101
Bands seen for the first time in 20+ years: 3
Bunches of flowers bought for Morrissey impersonator: 2
Punk icons spotted doing credible impression of World
    Cup-winning footballers: 1

In *The Last Don*, the final Mafia-themed novel of his to
be published while he was alive, *Godfather* author Mario
Puzo pondered the nature of regret and mortality. "What
is past is past," he wrote. "Never go back. Not for excuses.
Not for justification. Not for happiness. You are what you
are, the world is what it is."

I'm none too familiar with the vagaries of life as a body-dumping wise guy, but I do know that this slice of philosophy neatly articulates how I feel about bands reforming well beyond both their prime and their sell-by date. I'm willing to cut some slack to those on the bill at Rewind – they're all doing it with a knowing wink and often a sense of tongue-firmly-in-cheek high camp. But what of the more 'credible' outfits, those who populated the covers of the *NME* and *Melody Maker*? Those who only got played on Radio 1 after dark? Those who placed art well ahead of commerce? These principles have, in many cases, been overlooked second time around. There seem to be very few big fat cheques that can't magically smooth over previously insurmountable personality clashes and artistic differences. As that man Puzo again once told us, there are some offers you can't refuse…

Boston's Pixies are one of those – like Blur or The Stone Roses or The Libertines – who've bridged internal chasms in order to reunite. And their particular internal chasms were deep. In 1993, singer and chief songwriter Black Francis broke up the band. Two of the other three members were reportedly informed of his decision by fax. So when, 11 years later, they patched up their differences and started touring again, it was a move that gobsmacked many. Even more gobsmacking was the candour with which Black Francis, in a rather potty-mouthed diatribe to The Quietus website, rationalised the reunion.

"We're interested in anything that's going to earn us a fair wage," he railed. "It's not to say it's not about art, but we made that fucking art 20 years ago. So forget the fucking goddamn art. This ain't about the art any more. I did the arty farty part. Now it's time to talk about the money."

While I admire the bullshit-slicing rhetoric, I'm a little disturbed that this magnificent band – architects of such an original sound, authors of so many truly great rock'n'roll records, godparents of grunge – may have soiled their reputation by revealing themselves to be so keen about the folding stuff. Why are they happy to reheat past dishes, reluctant to come up with new recipes? When I was a kid, you'd pour scorn on the cheesy package shows of lesser-light '60s groups that still plied their trade in the Winter Gardens of out-of-season seaside towns, diluted versions of The Tremeloes or The Bachelors with a minimal number of original members. That was cabaret, that was showbusiness. It wasn't art. It wasn't what *your* favourite bands created. Now I'm worried that these bands have gone cabaret, gone show-business. Not in a seaside-special, kiss-me-quick hat-wearing kind of way admittedly, but still in a manner that suggests they've run out of ideas, that their best days are long past.

So I'm leaving my comfort zone of neatly filed memories. As well as making a date to catch the reassembled Pixies, I'm also going to check out another couple of favourites from my youth who've also got back together: The Wedding Present and Big Audio Dynamite. I'm travelling both near and far to see them – although, as none of them are playing a certain location in Essex, I'm sadly unable to call this chapter Look Back In Ongar.

Having originally seen all three first time around as the '80s slipped into the '90s, I'm risking some fondly held memories here. Memories like:

Pixies – Kilburn National Ballroom, London, 5 July 1989

Getting inexplicably lost between Kilburn Park Tube and Kilburn High Road, a beautiful *Caribou*, a bowel-shredding *Debaser*, an all-night café in Victoria, a ride on the 5am milk train home across the just-waking Home Counties.

Big Audio Dynamite – UEA, Norwich, 12 December 1989

An easily negotiated place on the guest-list, Mick Jones looking strangely younger than in his Clash days, a thick fog of (someone else's) marijuana smoke, a little too much Kronenbourg, some ill-advised 'dancing'.

The Wedding Present – Corn Exchange, Ipswich, 1 February 1990

A short minibus ride up the A12 with my university pals, a full-on mosh during the breakneck *Take Me*, a fruitless search for a post-gig bag of chips, a painful night's sleep with a suspected cracked rib.

I'm nervous about seeing all three bands again. I want my idols to remain youthful, not balding and haggard, tubby and unathletic. That's *my* job. But I do need to settle my inner unease about all these blessed reunions. They need to persuade me that getting back together again was a wise idea. Can there be a rebirth of cool?

First it's a date with those middle-aged Pixies. I'm riding the Docklands Light Railway eastbound towards Limehouse, where they're playing two nights in one of East London's less celebrated neighbourhoods. Venue and band are well suited. Troxy is a handsome art deco former cinema and bingo hall, recently refurbished as a live music venue and now reclaiming its former glory, a task Pixies will also be undertaking later tonight.

They're a favourite band of Jane's too, but she expressly declined when I offered to get her a ticket as well. Didn't want to know. She wants her perception of them to remain as it's always been, set in unmoving stone by that startling debut EP *Come On Pilgrim* and those four subsequent full-length albums. Here, as the driver-less train silently glides into Limehouse Station, I'm worried that she might be right. She usually is.

Judging by the crowds loitering on the pavement waiting for the doors to open, it seems that not many others share my unease about reunions. The touts are visibly frustrated. They can't get hold of any tickets for love nor money (OK, just money). One of them jabs me in the ribs in the chip shop queue, all West Ham tattoos and fistfuls of signet rings. He's noticed that I'm on my own, that a gig-going pal may have cried off, leaving a spare golden ticket unclaimed in my inside pocket. He's out of luck. I briefly consider stringing him along to see how deep into his own pockets his desperation makes him reach, but two things put me off: 1) the dirty looks of my chip-buying, Pixies-adoring brethren for appearing to deal with the devil; 2) the real possibility of mild-to-moderate physical violence.

Within the hour – chips demolished and touts departed – it's showtime. Pixies still look the part. Yes, there's been hair loss and Black Francis has put on way more than his fair share of middle-age spread, but they still ooze drop-dead coolness. And, launching straight into the surf-punk attack of the instrumental *Cecilia Ann*, they still sound like the exact same brakes-free juggernaut they always did.

Although the set is packed with familiar, crowd-pleasing songs, this excursion through the back catalogue is no pedestrian trundle. As much as Black Francis insists that it's all about the money, we're getting no supper-club performance tonight, even if, distressingly, the seats here in the front row of the balcony are arranged around little drinks tables. Kim the bass player frequently flashes her trademark cheerleader smile and engages in occasional sweet-voiced banter, but Black Francis remains an enigmatic force. He stays aloof, electing not to chat to the audience, instead evoking both the physical appearance of Uncle Fester from *The Addams Family* and the psychological menace of a dead-eyed serial killer. And when each song strikes up – *Debaser, Caribou, Wave Of Mutilation, Where Is My Mind?* – the four of them really inhabit it for the next three and a half minutes. The intensity, edge and mystery, which I felt so fiercely back in Kilburn in 1989, still burns.

With my ears still tingling with the last few mighty bars of final number *Here Comes Your Man* – and with further accompaniment from some distracting tinnitus – I head for the station. I've been proved wrong tonight. To be honest, I was won over rather easily, my defence as weak as that of a hungover Sunday morning football team on nearby Hackney Marshes. Even if I tried to play the chin-stroking, semi-detached *Late Review* pundit, deconstructing the performance as if it were a Degas exhibition at the National Gallery, the adrenalin shot of Joey Santiago's blowtorch guitar, plus the unabashed fervour of a venue full of hopelessly devoted acolytes, proved too seductive.

Reformed bands 1, Sceptic 0.

When it comes to making the most out of past musical glories, nowhere comes close to matching Liverpool. The city's international reputation is upheld not by one of its football teams winning the European Cup five times, but by its still-fervent promotion of its most famous musical sons whose heyday was half a century ago. If you played a word association game with the average Korean or Peruvian or Sierra Leonean and opened proceedings with "Liverpool", chances are they'd respond with "Lennon" or "McCartney", rather than "Keegan" or "Dalglish" (or even "Steve Ogrizovic").

The Beatles still run this town. Indeed, the very first thing I saw when I trotted down the steps of Lime Street Station wasn't the classical architecture of St George's Hall directly opposite, nor the somewhat less classical architecture of Radio City Tower. No, it was the largest digital billboard you've ever seen, upon which were beamed the youthful, grinning faces of Lennon, McCartney, Harrison and Starr, the space having been rented by Apple to announce the long-awaited availability of The Beatles back catalogue on iTunes.

Liverpool's unembarrassed embrace of music's heritage factor makes it the ideal place to catch up with The Wedding Present. So here we are, down in the bowels of the city's O2 Academy, just around the corner from the Liverpool Empire where posters grimly announce the arrival later in the year of Pamela Anderson in panto. David Gedge, forever the leader of The Wedding Present and the only original member remaining, cuts a commanding figure before me – over six feet tall and with a full head of jet-black hair. While he was never a stick-limbed indie softie like many of his contemporaries in the mid-'80s, in middle age he seems to have developed the stature of a swarthy, bone-crunching centre-half from the '50s, one who lined up for a muscular, no-nonsense team like Preston North End or Huddersfield Town.

Despite his imposing demeanour, David's only too happy to have a pre-gig chat, keen to put this latest chapter of the Weddoes' story into context. Having reconvened in 2004 after a seven-year hiatus, tonight they're revisiting their 1989 album *Bizarro*, playing it in its entirety. They've previously done likewise with their debut LP *George Best*, having been asked to play the album live by a record label who were putting out a 20th-anniversary reissue of it. It strikes me as a strange departure for a band that wear plenty of principles on their sleeves, such as refusing to do encores at their shows.

"It didn't really appeal to me at first," David concedes, sounding – in substance, if not accent – not unlike Clare Grogan at Rewind. "As an artist, you always want to look at the next thing. But to my surprise, I really enjoyed it. I found it quite an interesting experience to go back 20 years. You forget what you've learned. It was like reading an old diary. It sounds a bit philosophical, but I think I came to terms with the past being as important as the present and the future."

But what is it actually like as a fifty-something singing songs you wrote in your twenties? I know that I would retreat into the foetal position were I to clap eyes on something I wrote a quarter of a century ago, let alone recite it for a public audience. "It feels like I'm doing a cover version of someone else's song. I wouldn't have written them that way now, certainly. It's a horrible word to use in rock'n'roll, but my lyrics have definitely matured now. I look back at the early stuff and it's a bit like teenage angst – 'Oh my girlfriend's left me…'"

The Weddoes are far from the first to play complete albums live. Everyone from The Beach Boys to Public Enemy, Spiritualized to Steely Dan have been willing to reel in the years. Some don't limit themselves to just one album. Both Sparks and Kraftwerk have undertaken residencies where they play a different LP each night. Doing old albums live is a great defence against accusations of resigning yourself to looking to the past for inspiration. The recital of an earlier artistic statement becomes an artistic statement in itself, allowing the band to keep their integrity intact while covertly playing the lucrative nostalgia card. Having their cake and positively scoffing it too.

As well as being leader, singer and songwriter, David plays the role of road manager. (Indeed, he's rather interested in the deal I've got for myself tonight at the legendary Adelphi Hotel just down the road – a three-room suite, plus dinner and breakfast, all for £38. I kid you not.) But, while we're immersing ourselves in this haze of retrospection, he makes it clear that there's no rose-tinted fondness for the old ways of life on the road. "When we started, there were no mobile phones, no internet, no sat nav. All those things make touring a lot easier. Now there's no more finding a phone box and 'Have you got 10p?'. I used to have a suitcase of maps – of Berlin, Prague, Paris, wherever. Now everything's in the sat nav. There's no more 'Where are we?' at two in the morning. 'Is this a one-way street? It's too dark to read the signposts!' It doesn't always work, though. We wanted to find a Little Chef today, but it just took us to a field…"

An hour later, David has no problem finding his way to the stage where he leads his latest charges, who include the exotically named female bass player Pepe Le Moko. After half a dozen well-received numbers (including a rather fine new one called *End Credits*), the cheers grow threefold when, from beyond the grave, John Peel's voice intones, with all its unique inflections, "from the album *Bizarro*, this is *Brassneck*…". The place goes nuts.

Very soon, a group of around 20 of the more refreshed members of the crowd are doing their darnedest to start a mosh-pit. Now, I made a pre-gig promise to myself that tonight, should a mosh get underway, I'd be a willing participant, recreating all those times I've previously gone into battle, emerging an hour or so later with bruises galore and a suspected broken toe or two. I'm now breaking that promise.

I'm just too old. And poor. Not only have the bar prices stopped me from getting sufficiently refreshed to lose my inhibitions (maybe these moshers are those cash-rich hedge-fund managers whose bank balances we're all jealous of) but, frankly, by the time I'd get to the other side of the room to where the epicentre of the mosh is gathering strength, the song will be over. Best stay where I am. I've got a decent view, after all, and a cracked rib really does bloody hurt. And, presumably, takes longer to heal now that I'm 20 years older. It would rule me out of my weekly date on the five-a-side pitch for a good few weeks. And I'm not prepared to jeopardise my underwhelming role as the slow-from-the-blocks midfield general, huffing and puffing his way towards a cardiac arrest. So I'll just stay here on the sidelines, if you don't mind. I'm supposed to be the impartial observer, anyhow. Detachment at all times.

David Gedge is anything but detached. Focused and in the moment, 'perfunctory' clearly isn't in his vocabulary. In particular, his relentless playing on the high-velocity strumathon *Take Me* is extraordinary. I suspect not even the most muscle-bound, heavily tattooed thrash-metal guitarist can strum his instrument as fast and for as long as this eternal indie kid. "That'll be the death of me, that song," he quips as the song's last chord fades after nine minutes of fury. It certainly puts into the shade Brummie grindcore legends Napalm Death, whose most famous/ notorious song, *You Suffer*, lasts a full four seconds. Lightweights.

I'm among my own kind, tonight. The crowd is growing old with the band – we're almost exclusively male, almost exclusively born in the late-'60s/early-'70s and almost exclusively suffering from some degree of hair loss. David is one of the few people in the house with his barnet still intact, not that he's entirely relying on Mother Nature to keep his coiffure in fine fettle. "Do you dye your hair?" shouts a wag at one point. He answers in the affirmative.

Tonight, hearing *Bizarro* all the way through for the first time in years, I'm taken back to another time, another place. Two places, in fact: my pals Al and Phil's rented house at university (which could have been mistaken for the Colchester branch of The Wedding Present Appreciation Society), and my old Ents office on campus where the seven-inch of *Kennedy*, the first single off *Bizarro*, seemed to be spun on the hour, every hour. These aren't bad places to revisit. I'm starting to learn that treading on old ground doesn't disqualify you from also seeing yourself as a forward-looking, progressive-minded individual. I don't feel like I'm a hostage to hindsight, a prisoner of the past. The whole process actually feels liberating. A celebration, even.

Reformed bands 2, Sceptic 0.

If I'm surprised by the willingness of David Gedge to rewind time, I was always rather relieved that The Clash never quite managed to get the gang together for one last job. They almost did to mark their induction into the Rock and Roll Hall of Fame, but Paul Simonon exercised his veto, complaining that the ceremony's $2,000 ticket price "wasn't in the spirit of The Clash". And then Joe Strummer died suddenly, his death's only silver lining being that it put an end to the will they/won't they question. For me, they remain fixed in time.

But Mick Jones's most successful post-Clash band, Big Audio Dynamite, have done what Strummer et al didn't do. With all five original members signed up to the cause, BAD are now playing their first shows as a reconvened unit. I've arrived here, for their show at Bristol's O2 Academy, rather early. I was hoping to have a pre-gig chat with Mick and the band's second-lieutenant Don Letts to find out exactly why they've reformed. Certainly the decision seems at odds with a previous pronouncement by Don to *Billboard*: "I always think if you're lucky in life, you get a window of opportunity. Use it to the best of your ability and then fuck off and let someone else have their turn."

Our proposed chat was half-arranged through a mutual contact but, without a mobile number to fall back on, I'm not getting a sniff. I've asked several roadies to tell them I'm here.

"They're watching the racing," one of them relays to me.

"They're soundchecking now," reports another, ten minutes later.

"They've gone back to the hotel," explains a third after a further half-hour.

Harrumph. This is often the lot of the lowly music journo – especially one who didn't firm up plans beforehand. But I'm not alone. There's one other person here this early and it would be rude to stand next to her in silence. Hélène, a self-confessed serial early arriver, has flown from Paris just for the gig and has been standing here outside the venue since 4pm, a full three hours before the doors are due to open. But Hélène seems to deem even this level of advance planning insufficient. Leaving nothing to chance – and having spied the venue's "priority entrance for O2 customers" – she's gone and bought herself the cheapest available O2 phone so that she can make doubly sure that she's first in when the doors finally do open. And when they do, that prized position up against the stage barrier is hers – and with a new phone to play with until the main act comes on.

BAD hit the ground running, with the signature tune from *The Good, the Bad and the Ugly* and an opening toot on the harmonica announcing the still splendid-sounding *Medicine Show*. Not that they've blown their load too early. The well runs deeper than I remember and there are plenty of great tunes in their locker – *E=MC²*, *The Bottom Line*, *The Battle Of All Saints Road*, *C'mon Every Beatbox*...

Although reaching into the past tonight, Mick has never been one to rest on his laurels and live off former glories. He's always been eager to make new music, whether it's been his post-BAD outfit Carbon/Silicon, on those live appearances with Gorillaz, producing The Libertines' two albums or his work for Billy Bragg's Jail Guitar Doors project that takes music into Her Majesty's prisons. (A glance at Pete Doherty's charge sheet suggests those last two might not be unconnected.) But here, on the last night of the tour, it's not about the future. Mick's clearly enjoying peeling back the years, especially when he realises that tonight's venue used to be known as the Top Rank and was the scene of his last gig in England with The Clash.

And when he sings one particular line in *Medicine Show* – "Now if you're bald, it'll give you hair" – he can't resist a wry smile. The full head of hair he had during the Clash years, by turns spiky or bequiffed, has gone. In its place is what looks dangerously like a comb-over. With that and his thick-rimmed spectacles, one of the most important figures of the entire punk movement now shares more than a passing resemblance to an off-field Nobby Stiles. That wry smile isn't atypical tonight. Mick and the rest of them wear ear-to-ear beams throughout; after two weeks on the road together, they're clearly demob-happy. Don Letts bounds around the stage with all the zeal and agility of someone half his 55 years, those voluminous dread-locks just about constrained by his dark blue rasta hat.

The audience, the average age of which is somewhere between 35 and 50, are also clearly thrilled. Not that this means everything's safe and sanitised. At one point, just to my left, a scuffle breaks out. Although the incident ends up being more verbals than fisticuffs – perhaps they were just arguing over which Nicolas Roeg film was the source for a particular sample used in $E=MC^2$ – it does help to give the atmosphere that pinch of edge and danger otherwise missing from a venue that gives preferential treatment to those customers who've signed up for a phone tariff with a particular company. But, minor disagreements on the dancefloor aside, no-one seems to have an issue with these five ageing musicians retreading a path they last walked along decades ago. Least of all the singer and guitarist who, although he never managed it with The Clash, is perfectly at ease with a little time travel. "It's all about the five R's," he grins. "Reunion, reformation, relocation, restoration and resuscitation. Like your five-a-day."

I've enjoyed watching BAD every bit as much as I enjoyed watching Pixies and The Wedding Present. I'm not sure whether I really wanted to have such a good time. While I was cheered by my past heroes not embarrassing themselves on a public stage, I didn't necessarily want to be saluting their backward-looking stances. I'd prefer to be someone who hasn't turned his back on an unwritten future, who's not happy to snuggle under the comfort blanket of what's past and known. But it was hard to resist the allure of these shows. So what really is the difference between me taking gleeful pleasure in watching the acts of my youth and an older generation tucking into some chicken-in-a-basket and singing along to an exhumed '60s band in a cheesy country club? If I have swallowed the nostalgia pill, then maybe, as David Gedge suggests, it's possible – and, indeed, valuable – to be able to look in both directions. Forwards and backwards.

I might be confused, but there's no ambiguity about the score. 3-0 to the reformed bands. A conclusive victory. Never in doubt, was it? Ahem…

❀ ❀ ❀ ❀ ❀

Black Francis, David Gedge and Mick Jones might all have given sterling accounts of their 21st-century selves, but none of them ever quite occupied such a large part of my heart as the next band on my list. Not that the next band are, strictly speaking, the next band. Confused? Despite frequent rumours to the contrary, they're one of the very few not to have reformed since they split 25-odd years ago. They are, of course, The Smiths and tonight they'll be represented by proxy. A tribute band will be mimicking my heroes. I've got a bad feeling about this. A very bad feeling.

It's one thing to make peace with the middle-aged incarnations of your reunited favourite bands. It's quite another to be at ease with others taking the place of your personal saints. The Smiths occupy sacrosanct territory and anyone dabbling with their work is performing a sacrilegious act. And I'm going to be an accessory to the crime, probably struck down by some supernatural force simply by stepping over the threshold of tonight's show.

Like most music fans, I've always been scornful of tribute acts. I just feel that, if you've got the technical ability, go off and create something of your own rather than ride others' coat-tails. The most – and possibly only – interesting thing about tribute acts is their choice of name. There have been some crackers over the years, the best of which allude to the fact that they're replicating the originals. So take a bow the Faux Fighters, Oasish and, best of all, Earth, Wind For Hire. Another well-named act, the Bristol-based Rolling Clones, once actually received cease-and-desist letters from representatives of The Rolling Stones claiming breach of copyright, as if the earnings of a semi-amateur band capable of only half-filling the Fleece & Firkin could damage the income of another five-piece, one capable of completely filling Copacabana Beach with their adoring fans.

I've come up with a couple of belting names myself. Emerson, Fake & Palmer seems too good (or too obvious) a name not to have been used – but a quick Google search suggests it hasn't. Then there's The Disclaimers, an off-the-peg moniker that, in return for a reasonable finder's fee, I'll happily offer to any pair of guitar-toting, specs-wearing Scottish twins looking for a second income.

Tonight's tribute band, The Smiths Indeed (who share their name with a late-'80s fanzine), are currently sound-checking at Clwb Ifor Bach, a full-back's clearance from Cardiff's Millennium Stadium. First impressions, I reluctantly admit, aren't at all bad. They're running through *How Soon Is Now* and the guitarist has got that sighing riff down pat while 'Morrissey' is sounding pretty faithful and authentic. Guitars tuned and levels set, we head out into the city centre for a pre-gig omelette and chips. Well, three of the band and I do. 'Morrissey' excuses himself and heads off on his own, needing a little time to get into character.

Over the clink of cutlery and the squirt of the ketchup bottle, I first ask them about their career histories. They tell me they've been gainfully employed both as session musicians and in touring bands, often for artists from their home town of Liverpool. Bobby the bass player did five years with The Christians, while Paul the drummer has worked with self-proclaimed "full-time legend" Pete Wylie of Wah! fame. They've also had their own bands and written their own songs. So time for the $64,000 question: just when, and why, did they raise the white flag on their own creativity? It's a conundrum they're all eager to answer.

Bobby: Real life gets in the way. You need to pay the bills.

Simon the guitarist: You don't actually have to stop your creativity. I see this tour as the day job. I've got a studio in my house and I still write my own stuff. I've got no pretensions that I'm ever going to 'make it', but I still get a buzz from it.

Bobby: 'Making it' in my book is making a living out of music. So we're making it.

Paul: We still do sessions with famous people. But this is a job. Not every band can be the best band in the world. Not every songwriter is the best songwriter. But here we get to play songs we really enjoy playing, written by guys we really respect.

Simon: When you go to see an orchestra play Beethoven or Bruckner, that's a cover. But it's still as relevant today as it was then. I don't see why the music of The Smiths shouldn't be as relevant in the same way.

Bobby: There are certainly worse tribute bands to be in...

Being in a Smiths tribute band has a clear advantage. The demand to hear live Smiths songs will remain high all the while that the original band declines endless overtures to reform. (As I write this, that reunion is pencilled in for some time around the 12th of Never. Reader of the future, you of course may know otherwise.) Other tribute bands, such as the Abba-saluting Bjorn Again, have also prospered thanks to the dim prospect of the original gang getting back together, whether due to ill-fitting personality types or the premature arrival of the Grim Reaper. The Bootleg Beatles have now been in existence for more than 40 years; the lifespan of the actual Beatles was less than a quarter of that. Not that, as Simon points out, bands who pay tribute to outfits still performing aren't also making hay. "Ticket prices for the original bands are so expensive these days. There's a two-tier system. People are prepared to go and see a very good copy band, and have a good Friday night out, for £30 rather than spend £100, which is out of a lot of people's budgets." And, at best, the originals will only be playing at an out-of-town arena 60-odd miles away, rather than a venue in their home town.

"We're an advert for how good The Smiths were," declares Paul. "It's not our albums that people can go and buy. When a good tribute band visits town, its record shops sell more of the original records." Plus, Morrissey and Marr pocket a PRS payment every time The Smiths Indeed play a show. Meanwhile, the punters filling these venues seem unconcerned about the star turns being mere conduits of someone else's songs. "They're worshipping at the altar of The Smiths," says Simon. "That's what it feels like. They've all come together at the gig." Bobby goes one step further. "The songs are like sacred scrolls that have been handed down. OK, maybe that's taking it a bit far, but…"

The café owner turns the sign to 'Closed' and we head out. A Six Nations match-day makes Cardiff at 7pm look like any other city centre around midnight. Wales weren't even playing at home, but the all-day drinking is clearly taking its toll. The word 'carnage' will do nicely. On our way back to the club, Paul the drummer steers us towards the nearest Tesco. We're on a mercy dash for a necessary component of the live show of any Smiths tribute act – gladioli for 'Morrissey' to stuff into the back pocket of his jeans and wave in the air. Paul emerges with a couple of healthy-looking bunches, but is simmering. Tomorrow is Mothers' Day and the supermarket seems to have doubled its prices accordingly.

Back at Clwb Ifor Bach, the place is already almost full. Before the house lights go down, I make a quick, scientifically suspect headcount and am astonished. By my reckoning, no more than 15% of tonight's audience have yet seen their 30th birthday, meaning the vast majority wouldn't have been Smiths fans – or even alive – when the band was still active. I expected it to be a sea of balding pates where quiffs once flourished, but no. Tonight's crowd is far from the exclusive preserve of forty-somethings who've retrieved long-forgotten flowery shirts and saggy cardigans from the back of the wardrobe.

I approach one of these youngsters. Huw is a strapping lad in his late twenties from a village near Blackwood, Manic Street Preachers country. He discovered The Smiths just three years back but his conversion was instant. "I'll be driving home from work and hear a line and have to wipe a tear away. Lyrically, oooh…," he sighs. So it's not a problem that tonight's entertainment is a tribute act? "I just want to hear the songs live. Where else am I going to hear them?"

If twenty-somethings have tuned into the music of The Smiths a quarter-century on, perhaps Finn and Ned may do likewise in another decade or two. I'm rather glad Morrissey's songs still have a clear constituency, that they continue to articulate and explain youthful angst in the way they did to me. David Gedge's songs spoke to blokes who'd recently lost their girlfriends to the dullard down the street (*Everyone Thinks He Looks Daft* being the definitive text on the subject), but Moz's lyrics articulated the worries, concerns and collective despair of those of us who had yet to even ask a girl out, let alone experience the loss of her affections to someone else. The hills were very much alive with our celibate cries.

And by God does this new constituency know the songs. The band are recreating the *Meat Is Murder* album tonight and, a couple of minutes into opening number *The Headmaster Ritual*, the partisan crowd are glee-fully chanting lyrics about how "belligerent ghouls run Manchester schools". Even a song like *Jeanne* – a B-side from very early in The Smiths' career – is met with word-perfect accompaniment. I'm staggered. Huw was abso-lutely right. Who's playing these songs is less of a concern than hearing the songs themselves. It's not about the impressions, it's about the music. The evening becomes a communal celebration, a salute to Morrissey and Marr (and Andy Rourke and Mike Joyce too) made jointly by band and crowd alike. It certainly helps that the band do sound very, very close to the originators. The only inauthentic touch is when the bouncers swiftly neutralise any attempt at a stage invasion; in The Smiths' earlier years, Morrissey used to invite half the venue to get up and join him.

Although the others don't dress up as Marr, Rourke and Joyce, 'Morrissey' obviously needs to appear as Morrissey. He looks the part, aided by those expensive flowers poking out of his 501s, and vocally he's on the money, especially when it comes to between-song banter. At one point, the woman next to me taps me on the shoulder. "Is he miming?" she hollers above the middle eight of *That Joke Isn't Funny Anymore*. It's the ultimate compliment – and one that's all the more impressive seeing as how the singer's not from Morrissey's neck of the woods. Our doppelganger doesn't hail from Stretford, or anywhere else in Greater Manchester. He's not even a native of the north of England. His name is Jurgen and he comes from Belgium.

The shoulder-tapping woman might have been fooled, but in the men's toilets during the break, there is one dissenting voice. "It's a bit Smiths-by-numbers," grumbles one of the older audience members. His mate at the next urinal is bemused by the comment. "But they're a tribute band…" Still, this grumble was very much a minority view, as shown by the fullness of the audience's (largely) male voice choir that all but drowns out Jurgen's vocals during the second half of the show. I genuinely can't recall a gig, at least not for many years, where the audience has been so full-on, so committed. This night has opened my eyes.

It's the kind of adulation that a session musician would never otherwise experience. Seeing the tumultuous reception, I can now completely understand why Paul and Simon and Bobby and Jurgen spend their Friday and Saturday nights singing and playing other people's songs. And the attention doesn't end when they leave the stage. Afterwards, I briefly resume my roadie career, helping them carry the gear down the back stairs and out to their van. In the courtyard below, Jurgen is otherwise occupied. He's been detained by a bunch of delighted young men who want a photo opportunity. "Oi! Morrissey…"

I might not be asking for autographs, but I'm feeling just as buoyant. I expected to have my belief in the church of The Smiths dented by these false idols. Instead, my faith has been renewed in the most surprisingly evangelical way. And – ye gods! – it's a covers band who've done this to me. I must be mellowing.

But the mellowness is unlikely to last for long. I'll soon be leaving the sweaty bonhomie of after-dark Cardiff for more alien lands, off to a better-scented world of clinking glasses and picnic hampers. And, I strongly suspect, folding furniture.

5

WHERE THE WILD THINGS AREN'T

Destinations: Thetford Forest, Norfolk / Cornbury Park,
    Oxfordshire
Occasions: a concert among the pines / a Downing Street-
    endorsed tribal gathering
Miles travelled so far: 1,754
Items of garden furniture spotted: several dozen
Panama-hatted audience members: lost count somewhere
    around 30
Prime Ministerial walkabouts: 1

"Did you pack the cheese knife, Christine?"

As rock'n'roll quotations go, it's not exactly up there
with the Bob Dylan-baiting "Judas!" or The MC5's
instruction to "Kick out the jams, motherfuckers!".
Instead, it's the kind of enquiry you might overhear while
soaking up the sunshine on the manicured lawns of oper-
atic Glyndebourne.

This search for cutlery, at a pre-gig picnic, is indicative of the establishment's embrace of live music, of the degree to which rock has abdicated its rebellious, counter-cultural position. Were the punk wars really waged for the right to enjoy a multi-course, slap-up feed before the band came on? I fought the coleslaw and the coleslaw won.

But the overwhelming scene of civility opening out before me is, I have to admit, slightly reassuring. I've just passed through the heart of darkness – or, rather, driven three miles on dirt tracks through gloomy mist into the wild depths of Thetford Forest on the Norfolk/ Suffolk border. An unidentified orange warning light was lit up on the dashboard of my aged Honda, a possibly portentous sign of some evil lurking around the next foggy bend. But as the trees cleared and I reached journey's end, safe company was found. A cross-section of respectable Middle England has gathered for the purpose of a hamper-friendly, open-air concert from those poppy rocksters/rocky popsters – Keane.

As I park up, the paper plates and napkins are out in force, confirming that heavy and persistent drizzle will never get between an Englishman and his picnic. The Americans are the masters of this car-park-based self-catering, whether it's prior to a Green Bay Packers game or while the support act's on at a Jimmy Buffett concert. 'Tailgating' they call it, the tailgate of a pick-up truck being perfectly suited as an occasional table upon which to settle mountains of blackened animal flesh and kegs of underperforming American beer. The air will almost certainly be charged with exuberant hollering. Here in Thetford, the hatchbacks of East Anglia are hosting a more reserved affair. It's a Kettle-crisps-and-Applewood-cheese kind of occasion, the consumption of which is punctuated by conversation of the low-level, non-rowdy type.

Despite being way out in the sticks, it's not the country set who've gone down to the woods today. Suburbia has come out to play instead. Modest hatchbacks greatly outnumber the 4x4s, the outdoor attire of choice is Berghaus rather than Barbour, and the chinking glasses contain Chablis, not champers. They've driven on damp A-roads from the dormitory towns that dot these flatlands – Diss and Stowmarket, Wymondham and Bury St Edmunds. There are 7,000-odd of them too, so no doubt they've also come from further afield – the throbbing East Anglian metropolises of Norwich, Ipswich and Cambridge. In a region that's not exactly awash with venues capable of accommodating bands with Keane's pulling power, an hour's travel – or more – is never griped at. Expected even.

Cheese knife located and balsamic vinegar uncorked, the family parked in front of me start making a serious dent in their feast. Theirs is a spread rather more generous than my own: Walkers cheese-and-onion and one of those sugar-rush-inducing two-part giant Mars bars. They're a rather typical party this evening: couple in their late fifties, son on the cusp of 30 and prospective daughter-in-law politely laughing at prospective father-in-law's awkward stabs at humour. Keane's appeal clearly takes multiple generations in its embrace.

This has been something of a departure in recent years – going to a gig with your parents. I'd never have been seen dead at such an occasion with mine. (Sorry, Ma, but

I just wouldn't. Fortunately you never shared my love for fey, floppy-haired indie bands. They simply didn't cover enough Edward Woodward songs for your liking.)

I have a major problem with this shrinking of the generational divide. I'm all in favour of closeness between parent and offspring, bonds possibly articulated by supporting the same football team or by a shared love of fly fishing. But it's not supposed to exist when it comes to music. It's the great unwritten law of familial relations. Each new generation should be marking their own musical territory, creating a fresh soundtrack for their own particular life and times. Lines should be drawn and record collections mobilised. Then the battle for control of the family car stereo can commence, a bloody skirmish spiritedly fought between generations.

I think of Debra's daughters, singing their hearts out at Rewind. Kids are supposed to flee in the exact opposite direction of their forebears' record collection. I thought it was obligatory for teenagers to develop an addiction to the music of Joy Division or Slayer or Public Enemy, if only to repel the forces of middle-of-the-road evil seeping from their parents' stereos. Do the nation's staircases no longer resonate with cries of "Turn that racket down!" aimed towards teenage bedrooms? Is it more a case of "Oooh, that sounds nice. Do us a copy" instead?

It's probably no surprise that there's such an inter-generational crossover in record-buying and gig-going. Much of the blame can be directed at the backwards-glancing, retro-sounding nature of much of today's 'new' music. Parents like it because it sounds like Neil Young or Joni Mitchell or early U2 or The Human League. Their kids like it because it's made by youngsters just like them; they show little concern that it sounds date-stamped by a past age.

Digital music plays its part, too. An mp3 file shooting down the wire doesn't come with context-setting sleeve-notes; this absence further undermines even the flimsiest grasp of musical history. With everything available all the time, the ties to a specific era become loosened, some-times completely undone. We're witnessing the evapora-tion of embarrassment about sharing common ground with Mum and Dad's record collection. Or going to gigs with them.

Times have changed. My parents – and my friends' parents – never went to gigs. These took place in sticky-carpeted, subterranean dives of apparent vice and ini-quity, making them the perfect crucibles for the youth to articulate and display their generational angst. Or, more realistically, to play the quiz machine at the back whenever a duff band was on. My folks couldn't appre-ciate the thrill of these places. And they certainly never understood the appeal of sleeping on those cold railway station platforms.

But for the baby-boomer set that came along half a generation after my parents, live music became some-thing of a fixture of their social life. And, crucially, in the years since, it's never really ceased to be. This has always been familiar ground for them, since the time they sat cross-legged in teenage awe before Fairport Convention at the college hop or communed with Led Zeppelin through a haze of fragrant tobacco smoke at an early festival. And you don't need to be a highly decorated sociologist or statistician to work out that this is one of the key reasons for live music's growth. There are simply more people around who it not only appeals to, but for whom it's always had at least a semi-permanent place in their leisure time.

How different age groups are supposed to fill their time, and how they're supposed to behave, is no longer strictly delineated. Dads are just as likely as their teenage sons and daughters to spend an evening or two each week in their garage with their mates, behind a drum kit or turning everything up to 11. Similarly, fortysomethings who grew up in the age of the Atari and the ZX Spectrum can easily remain as obsessed by computer gaming as their offspring. And, with the PS3 or Wii otherwise occupied, the kids are upstairs blowing the dust off their parents' LP collections and learning the new and exotic art of placing needle onto vinyl. If 40 is the new 30 and 30 is the new 20, 20 can also be the new 40. The generational divide is narrowing in both directions. And, with it, out goes youthful rebellion.

Keane's tame, melodic songs ensure that, indeed, there's not the slightest hint of that youthful rebellion this evening. Picnics consumed, the remainder of that Chablis is now being decanted into plastic tumblers in observance of the arena's 'no glass' rule. It seems that, no matter how promptly Keane's fans pay their taxes or how honest they are when operating the self-scanning machinery at Sainsbury's, they still can't be trusted with glassware. I chuckle at a man who's having difficulty persuading one of the stewards that the tin of sardines he's packed in his hamper won't be hurled, with the pinpoint accuracy of a paratrooper's grenade, towards any of this evening's performers. And a 'no umbrellas' dictat is also being upheld by the otherwise genial stewards, despite the fact that the next few hours are going to be rather wet ones. My socks are already soaked through.

A couple of thousand umbrellas might be left behind in a couple of thousand car boots, but there are alternatives for keeping the rain out. The traditional fashions of the gig-going fraternity are conspicuous by their absence. No leather. No band T-shirts. No Converse boots or Doc Martens. There's even very little denim on display. Instead I'm being treated to a fashion show of outdoor wear that could tame the most Antarctic of conditions, outfits where everything but the eyes are shrink-wrapped in a coating of Gore-Tex. Neither Scott nor Shackleton ever felt the benefit of this clothing technology, but here it benefits these souls slowly trampling, stomachs comfortably full, on well-maintained, untesting forest paths. You suspect that, perhaps in little hidden pockets designed specifically for the very purpose, a bar or two of emergency Kendal Mint Cake might even be secreted – just in case some heinous misfortune befalls them on the couple of hundred yards from car to turnstile. Middle England does not come unprepared.

And Middle England doesn't come to the woods on a wet Thursday evening without a ticket, either. Accordingly, the touts are conspicuously absent, no-one offering the thrill of a minor black-market transaction. This is a tad annoying. Thanks to the kindly folk who handle Keane's publicity, I've got a spare ticket burning a hole in my cagoule pocket that will now go unused. A little extra cash could have compensated for the damp. Where's that West Ham-supporting tout from the Pixies show now that I need him?

But at least the touts' absence means they're not getting in the way of all these punters currently lugging some seriously sturdy folding furniture to the arena. Always prepared – and always in need of a little comfort too. A few have even brought duvets. Still, I'm disappointed that no candelabra can be spotted, no-one willing to raise the stakes on that time-worn lighter-in-the-air moment.

But, while reserving scorn for the picnics and the civility, I am quietly impressed by the location. The arena is gorgeous, a gently sloping clearing framed by dense, impossibly tall pines. As an outdoor venue for live music, it would be very hard to beat. Or, indeed, as a setting for a clear-sky, al fresco performance of *A Midsummer Night's Dream*. But tonight Titania's declaration that "The moon methinks looks with a watery eye" would be more fitting: the drizzly conditions are ruling out the chance of a single shaft of moonlight. Just low cloud and rain. However, dusk having descended, the twinkling lights around the arena try their best to compensate, and certainly give off something of the fairyland.

Praise – and a modest pay rise – should be aimed in the direction of the bright spark who came up with the notion of putting gigs in such a magical setting. So which cigar-chomping, feet-on-the-desk promoter is behind the concept? Well, it's not actually a traditional rock'n'roll impresario at all. The promoter of this evening's entertainment – and of similar evenings across this isle's woodland each summer – is actually the Forestry Commission itself. As live music has boomed, those beyond rock'n'roll's usual suspects have coveted a piece of the action, whether government department or stately home-owning, blue-blooded landowner. All are eager to cut themselves a slice of the live music cake – no more than a comparative sliver, but a cash-heavy one, nonetheless. And the Forestry Commission has found its own place on the bandwagon.

Mental arithmetic time. 7,000 tickets at £30 a pop is a tidy sum. There are also sold-out shows on the following two nights here at Thetford (headlined respectively by Simply Red and Doves), so multiply that original sum by three. And this series of woodland concerts is being replicated at five other Forestry Commission locations this particular summer, so that's some serious cash flowing into the coffers, fattening them up for the organisation's future work. Bearing in mind the coalition government's uncivil – and thankfully aborted – plan to sell off the nation's woodland to the highest bidder, anything that strengthens the Forestry Commission's hand is indubitably A Good Thing. And, as a method of fundraising, open-air concerts are infinitely more welcome than asking a squadron of student types to pounce on unsuspecting pedestrians, forcing them to walk in the gutter to avoid matey advances and requests for banking details.

Some non-financial brownie points are doubtless being scored at Forestry Commission HQ too. I'm envisaging a bank of filing cabinets, crammed with internal memos justifying these concerts through use of those buzzwords so worshipped by government departments and NGOs – 'inclusive', 'open', 'engage', 'accessible'. How 'inclusive' and 'accessible' these events actually are is, of course, another thing. Thirty pounds is a decent chunk of anyone's money, especially when the proceedings are far from weather-proof (and, let's not forget, umbrella-less). We're also some way into the forest here, well away from the sporadic support of public transport. It's a case of come by car or don't come at all.

This series of gigs comes under the accurate but dull banner of Forestry Commission Live Music. It's a shame that, having come up with a winning concept, they stopped short of giving it a remotely good name. But despite its prosaic moniker, the series has managed to entice some stellar acts into the nation's forests over the past few summers, among them Pulp, Paul Weller, Elbow and Massive Attack. For performers usually confined to anonymous city-centre venues and/or identikit edge-of-town arenas, these concerts offer something other than an indistinct repetition of the show the night before: a gigging memory that will endure. "Look at my cheeks," Jarvis Cocker announced to the Thetford crowd when he led Pulp here in a previous year. "I haven't had this much fresh air in years."

Things this evening are much more orderly and civilised than at those city-centre venues too. Those in the crowd who've brought their garden furniture are positioned halfway back up that gentle slope, rugs over their laps and family-sized bags of Werther's Originals handed up and down the line. All are waiting patiently, tolerating the support acts until Keane take to the stage. Even then, they show the same patience when hanging on for the band's big hits to be unleashed towards the end of the set. (If, that is, a sound as benign as Keane's can really be unleashed. Were music a dog, Keane would be a waggy, happy-to-comply cocker spaniel.) You get the sense that, were these hits delivered early on – or, indeed, were the support acts completely dispensed with – the rain-beaten, huddled masses would prefer an early exit. All wrapped up by ten and home in time for cocoa and *Question Time*.

Talking of cocoa, it's worth noting that the queue of the hot drinks stall is three times the length of that for the beer tent. The booze-sloshed, incident-heavy Reading Festival this is not. The police mooch around redundantly, patrolling without point or purpose, perhaps gagging to engage their batons on a juvenile squirrel that might have done something anti-social with a stray pine cone. What the forest's furry residents actually make of this musical invasion of their backyard goes unrecorded, although there's a strong chance that the orphaned offspring of the local deer that contributed to the Thetford Forest Venison Roast (£5 at the hot food concession) remain unimpressed.

My vegetarian sensibilities mean that the venison roast doesn't appeal. I can't say I go a bundle on Keane's music, either, but can appreciate how well it works outdoors, those big, broad choruses riding the air. The stage backdrop pronounces KEANE in 12-foot high letters. They might have picked a duff name as well, but it didn't slow the rapid acceleration of their career, nor the appeal of those open, instantly hummable melodies. And, when it comes to audience approval, it does no harm that the band aren't exactly chopsy, disagreeable crowd-baiters. "What a lovely bunch of people you are," singer Tom Chaplin declares at one point, all polite Home Counties enunciation. It's all so bloody *nice*.

When they play their biggest hit *Somewhere Only We Know*, you can almost see the collective – possibly smug – grin breaking out across the crowd as they realise the pertinence of the song to their current location, here in this secret forest clearing. As the chiming melody of *Everybody's Changing* then rings out, sleepy toddlers are reluctantly hoisted onto shoulders and encouraged to do the wavy-arms thing. Tipsy teenage couples canoodle, oblivious to – or uncaring of – the song's lyrics. "You're gone from here / Soon you will disappear."

Not everything's perfect. The sound at the back of the arena is rebounding off the pines. There's the bore of not being able to escape the cocoon of our wet-weather gear. And, to my ears, there's the music of Keane. But a few sprinkles of magic have been deposited here. I suspect it's probably just the effect of the surprisingly fine vegetable chilli nachos I scoffed half an hour ago, but I do reluctantly admit that there's something a bit special about this near-midsummer evening, an unarguable sense of decency at work.

Everyone is united by the music, by the beautiful surroundings, by the more-than-adequate toilet allocation. Mark King's words at the Rewind Festival, about the unifying, spiritual force of live music, ring true. Here in this cathedral of pines, we're given a sense of what England could and should be, a cynic-bashing love letter to this sceptred isle, a cockles-warming riposte to bad-news Britain.

And then it takes an hour and a half to get out of the car park.

※ ※ ※ ※ ※

If Thetford Forest hadn't quite got its traffic measures sorted, it's a different matter now, here in the rolling Cotswolds. I'm perched on the back of a golf buggy, speeding downhill 'twixt car park and VIP arena. Despite the odd bump, it's an agreeable way to travel, even if it's only the shortest of hops. It appears that the VIPs here at Oxfordshire's Cornbury Festival are much too 'very important' to actually walk the mere 300 yards under their own steam.

I say it's an agreeable way to travel, but I'm trying to shut out the boorish tones of my fellow buggy passengers, all of whom appear to be local Tory party volunteers trying to outdo each other with their electioneering anecdotes. "Did you get that email from Dave yesterday? You didn't?! Yes, 10.34 in the morning. That's when mine arrived." (We'll meet "Dave" a little later on.)

Where the Keane audience was suburban in composition and outlook, Cornbury sends out a hearty call – and I'd like to imagine it was sounded by a huntsman's bugle – to a more landed, more monied constituency. Not for nothing has Cornbury been dubbed 'Poshstock', a label that any other festival would retreat from on the swiftest of heels. But not Cornbury. This is an event that positively rejoices in its nickname, subverting the sneers as it gratefully receives some perfect, one-word branding on a plate.

And, judging from the fleet of 4x4s and straight-off-the-forecourt convertibles outclassing my dirty Honda in the car park, posh it certainly is. But it's not just the mode of transport telling me this. Another way you can evaluate the refinement of a festival is by its VIP area. Some gatherings refuse to offer such accommodation; others, embarrassed that doing so would be at odds with their outward projections as egalitarian, all-in-it-together bashes, hide the area away within a labyrinth of high fencing. (Not that festival VIP areas are usually anything worth hiding, of course. They're simply places where the loos have a nicer odour. Or, at least, where the loos don't smell quite as eye-strainingly putrid as those on the punters' side of the fence.)

But there's no such sense of social embarrassment here at Cornbury. Discretion seems to have been well and truly dispensed with. The VIP tent, a huge marquee around which bunches of noisy types in Panama hats are congregating, sits right in the heart of the festival. This is an event that displays its social hierarchy in the most conspicuous way. The not-so-important people – that is, those who haven't forked out extra cash for VIP status – are given a pretty clear view of what's beyond their privileges, of the inner sanctum lying just the other side of the knee-high white picket fence that marks the dividing line.

I nose around the marquee to see what they're missing. And what they're missing is, admittedly, highly civilised. Inside is all manner of squashy furniture – lots of bamboo and hessian. And little bowls of nuts and nibbles (with which, ever the freeloading music hack, I fill my pockets). It's all very John Lewis. Indeed, it's very much the kind of arrangement that Colonel Gaddafi would probably have held court in whenever he fancied a foray into the desert. As outdoor accommodation goes, it's hard to imagine that anything comes much more sumptuous than this.

But don't worry about the underlings. Cornbury's lower orders aren't exactly slumming it on the other side of the picket fence. They're busy refuelling themselves at Jamie Oliver's food stall or in cocktail bars run by that bastion of upper-middle-class domestic bliss – Waitrose. There's the obligatory pig roast (always an unwelcome and undignified sight for us veggies) while, at the top of the field, overenthusiastic bar staff in a double-decker bus are dispensing endless pitchers of Pimms. Young girls, angel wings fixed to their shoulders, float by in what must be to them some brightly coloured, sun-drenched wonderland.

It's all extraordinarily respectable. The local primary school is even hosting the cake tent.

This scene – of a well-heeled garden fete with added live music – couldn't look more English. Or, at least, it's a notion of Englishness that's alleged to be the universal experience, the kind of skewed and exaggerated portrait of a nation's leisure time painted by the films of Richard Curtis in order to pocket a wad or three of American box-office dollars. Funnily enough, Curtis is no stranger to Cornbury. He was here a few summers back, down the front with local MP David Cameron when Echo & The Bunnymen were on. No, really. Stop sniggering. And delete that mental image of powder-blue cashmere sweaters tied with deliberate dishevelment around their shoulders. Perhaps his attendance was all in the name of research. If so, expect another Curtis-penned rom-com – the central plot of which revolves around the will-they-won't-they courtship between an itinerant American songstress and a bumbling Cotswold dairy farmer – to be cramming them in at your local multiplex any time soon.

Cameron, the "Dave" so glowingly referred to by my fellow golf-buggy passengers, is making a return visit to Cornbury this weekend, but in an altogether different role. No more the off-duty local MP claiming to have a half-decent record collection. He's since become the Prime Minister, no longer able to idly wander the site with wife and children. He now strides with arrow-straight purpose, moving through the fair flanked not by family but by around a dozen members of the security services. Just like Prince Charles on the Pyramid Stage at Glastonbury, Cameron knows what good photo opportunities such events make. A photo on a couple of front pages will surely be his tomorrow. This intersection of Downing Street and live music would never have happened in my day. Margaret Thatcher pogoing at Dingwalls to Peter & The Test Tube Babies? John Major throwing some off-his-bonce shapes to The Shamen in some abandoned warehouse? Only in my wildest, cheese-fuelled dreams.

Despite all the attendant festival infrastructure – what the poet Simon Armitage neatly refers to as "fringery" – and the presence of the PM, there is still that feel of the garden fete about Cornbury, albeit one offering the optional extra of overnight camping in the lower paddock. The bands it books might not be the latest Hoxton-approved darlings of the music press (indeed, most are on the slow downhill stretch from their career peaks), but they've not been dredged up from the bargain-bucket C-list either.

Just over there, why, isn't that dapper-dressed chap Muddy Waters' old sidekick Buddy Guy? Listen closely. Isn't that the deliciously honeyed voice of soul diva Candi Staton – last heard going up against Kelis at Glastonbury – filling the air to our left? And now, wafting over a few thousand heads, here come Squeeze with an impeccable version of *Pulling Mussels (From The Shell)*, surely the finest moment in their voluminous back catalogue.

The Cornbury line-up – its quality in particular – flags up the event's biggest problem. It suffers from something of an identity crisis. This is a festival that clearly would like to be more than it is. And in trying to punch above its weight, the quantity of 'name' acts it books is too great for its existing audience, a large proportion of whom I'd guess are casual onlookers here for the overall occasion rather than to noisily demand a live version of an obscure early B-side from whoever's currently on stage.

On the flipside, the acts the festival does book aren't quite cool enough to attract a musically devout audience. So, for the Cornbury crowd as it currently stands, Squeeze are the perfect booking – a band with enough Top 20 hits to draw upon to snag the interest of the floating voter. David Gray likewise. The Blockheads, too. No problem there. Everyone knows the handful of big hits that each has had.

But not all acts hit the mark. Often the confluence of crowd and performer at Cornbury is an awkward fit. I've arranged to meet up with my pal Mark Ellen, the former *Whistle Test* presenter and my editor at *The Word* magazine. He texts me: "See you at 6.30 by Dr John's mixing desk". Mark's a bona fide festival veteran, from the mud-heavy, comfort-light rock gatherings of the early '70s onwards. He knows full well that, when meeting up with friends at a heavily populated festival, you need to avoid a never-ending game of Where's Wally? Accordingly, he invariably wears a fluorescent yellow cycling jacket on such occasions, one that's probably visible from an adjacent county. He's wearing it today and I spot him immediately.

But he needn't have bothered. We'd have easily found each other anyway – the crowd is very sparse around Dr John's mixing desk. Indeed, this mixing desk is not serving the main stage; it's set up for the much smaller stage further up the hill, beyond the beer tent and all the food stalls. Greetings exchanged and pints raised, Mark and I head closer to grab a better view of the wizened old New Orleans piano master. It's not a difficult task. The crowd is wispy and we casually saunter right up to the front row. People should be sharpening their elbows and jostling each other to get such a prime spot from which to witness such an important figure in popular music history. But the Cornbury crowd don't seem to care. Instead, the allure of the on-site creperie seems to hold greater sway. This is a music festival where music doesn't appear to be the principal reason for attendance.

That Dr John – or, for that matter, Candi Staton – are not appearing on the main stage does suggest that Cornbury is oversupplying its punters. And this, rather sadly, is born out a few months later when Cornbury Music Festival Ltd slides into liquidation, having failed to turn a profit in any of its seven years of existence. The company reportedly owes a chunk of money to Lord and Lady Rotherwick, the festival's landlords here at 6,500-acre Cornbury Park. Other listed creditors include performers from past years – Crowded House were reported to still be owed more than £15,000, while Paul Simon's pockets remained light to the tune of a whopping £33,000.

It's not that Cornbury is put together by innocent country bumpkins getting fleeced by the fees that agents in London are charging them. The festival is the baby of Hugh Phillimore, an Old Etonian who's been in the music business for more than 30 years. He's an experienced man, undoubtedly a player. Another of his companies, Sound Advice, has a rather enviable – and, you'd imagine, rather profitable – line in procuring the absolute top A-list singers and musicians to play at private parties. If you're a Russian oligarch and you want Christina Aguilera and Enrique Iglesias to play at your wedding, Hugh's the man to call. (This is a commission he's fulfilled. He also provided the entertainment for both Elton John's nuptials and Prince Charles's 50th birthday.)

But, despite newspaper headlines announcing live music's recession-proof qualities, Cornbury's far from an all-out success. It once was. A festival ran on the site for 60 years until the middle of the 19th century, but ended when it became too popular. The irony won't be lost on Hugh Phillimore, but he's got plans. Having linked up with the promoters of the X Factor live tours, he's packing the Cornbury Festival name into his 4x4 and driving it a few miles up the road to another country estate.

I won't be in a hurry to follow. I might be firmly entrenched in middle age, but I'm still not ready for these kinds of events yet, where passion is low and musical appreciation comes a distant third to social posturing and Pimms intake. Hopefully I won't ever be ready for them.

Instead, I've got a date elsewhere, a destination a world away from picnic hampers and Panama hats and Tory Party volunteers. A place where the pulse is strong, the passion pure. Bring the noise.

6

RUN TO THE HILLS

Destination: Catton Hall, Derbyshire
Occasion: Bloodstock metal festival
Miles travelled so far: 2,034
Number of festival-goers older than me: approx 4
Hours of sleep in a wet, mud-coated tent: 0
Hours of sleep in a dry, warm B&B: 8.5

Black, black, black. It's all I can see, it's all I can hear. The sky is crammed with bible-black clouds. The land is occupied by a mass of black-shirted, black-trousered, black-booted music fans. And the air is thick with the blackest sounds ever voluntarily made by a human being. Who could have guessed that this tableau was being played out in the grounds of a stately home in the heart of Middle England in high-summer August? Welcome to Bloodstock.

It's one thing to invite a well-behaved, family-friendly festival like Cornbury to set up shop on your front lawn. It's quite another to open the gates of your estate to a massed invasion of metal bands and 10,000 of their hardcore acolytes. But that's exactly what has happened here in the bottom corner of Derbyshire, just where the county snuggles up to Staffordshire and Leicestershire. The grounds of Catton Hall, normally host to sedate equestrian events and dog trials, are currently vibrating to a degree that could surely register a decent reading on the Richter scale. Past the elegant 18th-century red-brick house and across the lawns that run down to the meandering River Trent, the ground is rapidly turning from its usual lush green carpet to a sticky tiramisu of mud as bands rejoicing in the names of Cannibal Corpse, Bloodbath, Obituary and Onslaught bring the gospel of metal to this sedate corner of the East Midlands.

I know I was craving music with passion, but, shit, I don't think I'm ready for Bloodstock to convert me just yet.

This is a festival that's the polar opposite of Cornbury. For starters, that bucolic golden glow is absent. Someone's shot out the lights. These sooty, ominous skies are, of course, entirely appropriate. Dazzling sunshine just wouldn't do the music justice. Rather neatly, today is also Friday the 13th.

There's no prime-ministerial walkabout here, no local school running a cake stall. Indeed, one of Bloodstock's concession stands, offering 'metal makeovers', appears to be called Satan's War Forever. (I bet it was an amusing day at Companies House when that name was put forward for registration.) Elsewhere, swap Cornbury's Pimms-decanting double-decker bus for a decommissioned US army truck, rebadged as a Jagermeister bar. And, for all those boutique festivals offering sweeter-smelling 'posh loos', here at Bloodstock open-air urinals are indiscreetly placed right slapbang in the middle of the main drag for all to witness.

There are no shoe-saving golf buggies, either. Instead, it's a reassuringly muddy half-mile trudge from car park to festival site. Just as it should be, really. There's plenty of the festival purist in me, so I'd heartily agree with those who claim that your festival weekend will ultimately be more satisfying if you suffer a little here and there. In the age of the fully equipped boutique festival, where a minor disaster has occurred if the organic bread stall is offering fewer than three different focaccia loaves to choose from, rough-and-ready Bloodstock appears to be an occasion worth anyone's applause. Its punters seem to just get right stuck in.

When the rains come, the faithful barely notice it; there's no mass retreat to the warm and dry bosom of a chai tent. Bloodstock is simply a continuation of an older-style, no-nonsense festival spirit where the pain of a few hours' back-wrenching sleep in the most basic of tents can be anaesthetised by cracking open a four-pack of budget lager at ten the next morning.

I think back to that morning when, on the way back from school, I hit upon the idea of this road trip. I smile a little smile. This is a festival whose choice of head-liner will never be discussed on the *Today* programme, a tribal gathering that's never going to be the subject of a ticket promotion on the back of a cereal packet. For those of us a little mistrustful of the mainstream's over-whelming embrace of live music, this is a good thing. Some things need to be clung on to. The bathwater might have drained away, but we're holding on tight to the baby.

And although I'm proud of myself for pushing at the limits of my comfort zone, there's no denying that I'm not at home here. I'm aware that I'm pretty damn conspicuous. I have no piercings. I'm without tattoos. I have no unruly, unwashed mop of hair cascading down my shoulders (quite the opposite, sadly). I haven't even plumped for the de rigueur black clothing. Instead, I'm wearing the everyman uniform of the on-location music journalist – crumpled checked shirt, combats and a pair of Adidas trainers. Suede trainers, at that. These are shoes that, in the least surprising event in the history of unsurprising events, instantly prove woefully inadequate for the conditions and take a serious battering on my very first skate across the mud.

As much as I'm a battle-hardened festival veteran who's seen plenty of action in the bleakest, Somme-like conditions, I've let myself down here. People must think I'm some kind of wet-behind-the-ears novice. Where are those sturdy, mud-repelling walking boots? I know exactly where they are. Next to the bedside table in the cosy B&B back in Tamworth. I slipped out of them to enjoy a pre-Bloodstock hot chocolate and one of those little packets of custard creams.

I don't need to be a mind-reader to know exactly what you're thinking. You may have already thrown this book down on the floor in disgust and therefore aren't reading these very words. Hardened festival veteran? Cosy B&B? Yes, *I know.* The two things should be incompatible, never the twain should meet, etc. But, but… Yes, I'm supposed to be getting my groove back. Yes, I'm supposed to be searching for the heart and soul of live music. But I figure that, if I haven't achieved that in ten, rain-sodden hours here at Bloodstock, I'm unlikely to find it by spending a few additional hours under canvas while a procession of mud-caked, herbally relaxed teenagers stumble and fall on my tent. And, besides, there's a good film on later if I'm back in Tamworth in time. And I'm certainly in no hurry to turn down the offer of a decent breakfast and the weekend papers come sunrise...

Going native is no prerequisite for this road trip. Well, not where Bloodstock's concerned, that is. I'm not going to pretend to be any younger than I am. I'm fully aware that, to the gathered faithful, I must surely be here in a fatherly capacity; someone who, having accompanied his 15-year-old, has been instantly jettisoned on arrival as Junior charged off to the main stage throng, leaving Pop to wander around the site with a quizzical, lost look on his chops.

My mind spins forward a dozen years and I say a little prayer that neither of my two lads ever become metalheads. Yes, more hypocrisy. I know this is completely at odds with what I said back at that Keane show about youngsters' music tastes needing to be self-determined and independent of those of their parents, but I'll take any criticism squarely on the chin. The thought of our house's foundations being shaken by the unholy sound of metal for several years is simply too heinous to consider.

A text arrives from Jane. Apparently it's a glorious day back in Somerset. She and the boys are currently enjoying a cream tea at a local castle. Jealous? Just a bit. Here I am, trying to find the slightest patch of shelter, under which I can jot down a few observations in a soggy notebook. For those festival-goers who might not have assumed I was here on chaperoning duties, my fevered scribbling possibly marks me down as a plain-clothes copper. Maybe an undercover drugs squad officer commanded by his superiors to wear his civvies in order to seamlessly blend in with the surroundings.

Or, most likely, not a single soul is wondering what I'm doing here. No-one, after all, seems distracted from the task at hand – Bloodstock is ALL about the music. There are very few distractions. To get to the heart of the matter, I head off to witness events from the closest of quarters, squeezing into the photographers' pit between band and acolytes with my notebook at the ready. Experimental metallists Meshuggah are just taking to the stage. If the heard-in-the-next-county roar that welcomes them didn't give you enough of a clue, the level of these Swedes' popularity can be measured by the steady stream of crowd-surfing human traffic being scooped over the front barrier by the security crew. Fair play to the stewards who all remain cheery throughout, even when one serial offender refuses to give them any respite. He must have gone over the top a dozen times. The odd bottle is making its way over the barrier too so, without hanging around to check whether they're filled with wee or not, I retreat to the relative calm of the backstage area. Ten minutes in the pit was more than ample.

Backstage at festivals is usually a dull old place, a jumble of Portakabins populated by uninterested performers idly pushing some lukewarm food around a paper plate while they wait for showtime. But Bloodstock's backstage area is the first I've ever visited that's laid on its own tattooist/"pierce artist" (geddit?) – perfect for any of today's star turns who might have a spare inch of skin that needs either colouring in or having a sharp needle stuck through it. Although I could possibly do with blending in a little more, I resist the tattooist's kindly advances.

Instead I try to track down Paul Gregory, the guy who co-founded the fiercely independent Bloodstock ten years ago. I expect to encounter someone with a wild mane of hair, a gallery of tattoos on every limb and a half-drunk bottle of Jack Daniels in his grasp. Probably a fine line in big-talking hyperbole, too. Instead I find myself shaking hands with a chap on the cusp of 60 who, with his glasses and neat goatee, looks more like the boss of a modest IT company. As the rain starts to get heavier, Paul offers shelter in the cab of his Bloodstock-branded pick-up truck. It's here that he tells me about the event's origins.

An artist by trade (one whose interpretations of Tolkien's Middle Earth have graced the walls of both Sotheby's and the Barbican), Paul stumbled into festival promoting when he and an associate discovered that they shared a love of metal. Spotting a void in the market around the turn of the millennium, the pair launched an indoor festival in Derby. "It had a capacity of around 2,500 but we only had about 600 or 700 people for that first one. So we lost money on that. But it was an investment and it just developed from there. It's been an eye-opener. I was completely out of my depth, but I think that was the best way to do it. For our first open-air festival, the stage was leaning to the left, then it got struck by lightning..." A smile. "You couldn't make it up."

When the festival moved outdoors, it was comparatively easy to persuade the Neilson family, the owners of Catton Hall, to host it. "Robin Neilson's a great character and just said 'Yes'. I don't think he actually understood what he was in for. But he grew with it. We tried to placate him by making sure that his house wasn't invaded or anything. He's invited his entire family to come down this year. I think he loves it. Well, he either loves the festival or he loves the money!"

After ten years, Bloodstock stands proudly independent, having carved itself a place that complements the heavier-hitting metal festivals. "We have a niche in the market. We don't want to go for the Iron Maidens, the bigger metal bands. If you get a big-hitter, who do you get next year? You create a problem, year on year. So we bring over lots of bands who've never played the UK before – that's always been our niche. We can't compete with the big boys like Sonisphere or Download, even if we wanted to. They'd crush you if they felt the need to."

I have unsullied respect and admiration for what Paul and his small team have achieved with Bloodstock. It's an event born out of a devotional love for music, its original inspiration never that of providing a decent bottom line on a balance sheet. Instead, it provides one of the red-letter weekends of the year for the 10,000 souls gathered here. Overseas aid workers aside, there can be few ways of achieving such job satisfaction, no matter what your trade.

Bloodstock's mantra – "By fans for the fans" – is no empty marketing slogan. "Our ethos has never been about making huge amounts of rent," says Paul, "and I think the fans see it this way." The festival ploughs money into the Unsigned Stage where the better acts drawn from a good old-fashioned nationwide Battle of the Bands competition find themselves on the Bloodstock bill. Paul sees this as all for the long-term greater good of the metal massive. Furthermore, rather than sell the naming rights of its stages to a mobile phone company or drinks manufacturer, the Bloodstock team (several of whom have been recruited from Paul's immediate family) opt for something infinitely more honourable. One of the tents is called the Sophie Lancaster Stage, named in tribute to the young goth murdered by a gang in a Lancashire park in 2007.

Commendable stuff. Principles are often in short supply in the music industry, after all, a place where stories of cut-throat, capricious shenanigans are legion. Celebrated, even. But, while I admire Bloodstock's idealism and its refusal to bank the corporate buck, I do have a little problem with its music. Without wishing to sound like the out-of-touch, middle-aged father that I of course actually am, I have genuine difficulty discerning between most of these bands, the majority of whom appear to hail from various points across Scandinavia. It's not simply a language barrier I'm unable to surmount – most of the frontmen's screams appear not to be in any language spoken on this planet. I simply can't tell my Meshuggah from my Gorgoroth. To apply that infuriating phrase used by generations of parents, it all sounds the same. I'm sorry. It. Just. Does.

The 10,000 people before me in this field would probably lamp me on the spot for such a woefully ill-informed generalisation. And rightly so. After all, I pride myself on knowing a wee bit about African music – my parlour piece would be being played ten African records and correctly identifying the country of origin of at least eight of them. So, to me, it wouldn't seem unreasonable to want to slap anyone unable – or who simply couldn't be bothered – to spot the difference between some horn-heavy Nigerian

Afrobeat and a little unaccompanied balafon playing from Guinea. They just need to try harder.

I need to try harder too, but metal is a confusing business. A great many branches have sprouted from the gnarled trunk of what, in less complicated times, was simply referred to as heavy metal. There's black metal, death metal, thrash metal, doom metal, drone metal, metalcore, industrial metal, Viking metal, Southern metal, neo-classical metal, post-metal, gothic metal, sludge metal...

Paul Gregory asks me if I like the music. Rather than giving him the honest answer ("the most musically depressing experience of my life" is a phrase that's been on the tip of my tongue all afternoon), I plump for a fence-straddling "It intrigues me". He seems at least partially placated. And it does intrigue me – just what does this music contain to invoke such a spiritual reaction among its fans? It would be easy merely to poke fun at it, after all – the synchronised, non-ironic head-banging; the relentless sea of hands making those ubiquitous 'devil horn' gestures; the stream of men old enough to know better who've raided the kitchen cupboard for flour and food colouring in order to resemble an extra from *The Evil Dead*.

But, despite my inability to understand the music and its appeal, I can't scoff at the sense of community. Bloodstock might not be about diversity or variety, but it is a fellowship, united by an overwhelming, curiously endearing love for this narrow strain of music. And, despite the rain and the noise and the muddy gloop that formed inside my trainers several hours ago, I actually feel more comfortable here than I did in Thetford Forest or at Cornbury. Neither had the passion and spirit that's in abundance here. I still consider each Bloodstock turn to be making a godawful racket, but I also applaud this crowd of largely suburban teens and young twenty-somethings for not being the kind of kids happy to share a picnic with their parents at a Keane gig. Instead, these are people who care deeply about their music, who are defined by it, who are sufficiently committed to put up with whatever conditions are thrown at them in the pursuit of it. They don't need a literary tent or an artisan bread stall. And that's more than commendable to me. For those here to rock, I salute you.

And, at their heart, they're a placid bunch too. Bloodstock matches the trouble-free proceedings of Thetford and Cornbury; there's not a whiff of malice in the air, as Paul notes. "The music's aggressive, but the people are peaceful." Which is just as well. A man brushes past the pick-up truck, a perfect replica of Leatherface from *The Texas Chainsaw Massacre*. We dissolve into giggles. "That's quality, isn't it?" chuckles Paul. Thankfully the peace remains unbroken. It did, after all, appear to be a real chainsaw he was carrying. It certainly wasn't a cheese knife.

7

THIS MUST BE THE PLACE

Destinations: Eigg, Inner Hebrides / Butlin's, Minehead
Occasions: The Fence Collective's Away Game / All Tomorrow's Parties
Miles travelled so far: 3,206
Modes of transport: 5
Packets of Cheddars scoffed: 7
Curry buffets consumed: 2
Near-death experiences: just the one

Of all the gigs I've been to, no matter how insalubrious the venue, its security staff or clientele, I've never felt that my life was in danger, that I was just approaching the midnight hour of my existence. But God, I'm feeling it now.

Several things are suggesting my time is nigh. Firstly, that this boat is tipping up violently, before crashing back onto the dark waters, giving a view of sky, then sea, then sky. Then sea. Then some more sky. Secondly, that this boat is also lurching left to right, pivoting wildly like some perfectly engineered fairground ride – with the added 'thrill' of the unforgiving depths below. And, finally, that the boat's captain, a man called Ronnie who generously agrees that it is "a wee bit splashy" today, is having to cut the engines every time a particularly bad wave approaches. They all feel bad to me.

The weather didn't suggest it would be like this. Fifteen minutes ago, it was a benign, sunny afternoon when this compact boat, the *Sheerwater* – normally commissioned for placid wildlife excursions here on the waters of the Inner Hebrides – left the small port of Arisaig en route to a music festival on the island of Eigg.

That's Eigg, just over there. It doesn't seem far, does it? Yet here we are, going through hell and high water to reach its shores. 'We' are the 80-person cargo, the third shipment of the day heading for the Away Game festival, as organised by Fife's Fence Collective. We were a jolly bunch as we left our snug harbour, popping open cans and handing around bottles of rum and whisky in joyful anticipation of the weekend ahead.

Even when we reached open seas and the first splashes came overboard, we were simply a bunch of schoolkids on the log flume ride at Alton Towers. But that giddy laughter is now hollow and nervous. Those 'open seas' weren't the real 'open seas'. These ones are. And don't our internal organs know it.

Aside from this boatful of festival-goers (many of whom sport thick beards, unnecessarily adding to the cargo's weight), there's a hell of a lot of camping gear stowed down in the hold. Now, I'm no sailor but I imagine, with that load on board, we'd go down like a stone. A boulder, in fact. A bloody great fast-sinking, boat-shaped boulder.

I'm presuming there are some life jackets stashed around here somewhere – if so, I must have missed the safety announcement telling us where they are. Another large swell, then the inevitable crash of hull on water a second or two later. God, these waves are big – parabolic, in fact. (Although, when I later file my report on the Away Game for *The Sunday Times* and use "parabolic" to describe the conditions, the fact-checking sub-editor suggests that the waves of a Force 6 squall are more "rocking" in their nature, so "parabolic" falls victim to the delete button. Harrumph.)

I feel a sudden rush rise through my legs, then up through stomach and chest. A hastily requested carrier bag collects my reconstituted mid-afternoon snacking. "Better out than in," I hear someone comment, and I look up to see all the other passengers looking back at me, a sea of faces united in sympathy and solidarity. Several kindly offer anything that'll improve my condition – water, whisky, chocolate...

I feel the colour drain from me and sink my forehead onto the welcoming cold metal of a door handle. Drifting in and out of consciousness, my head swirls with an old folk song called *Annan Water*, recently revived by Oregon indie-folk outfit The Decemberists – "Calm you waves and slow the churn/You may have my precious bones on my return."

And when my brain's not repeating that cheery refrain, it's busy trying to estimate how much it would cost to charter a helicopter to get me the hell off that craggy island at the end of the weekend. I can't – *can't* – go through this boat ride again.

Dreams of comparatively safe helicopter travel disperse after about 40 minutes. The swell has subsided and my fellow passengers are calm and happy again. Laughter has returned. We're here – and we're alive! The *Sheerwater* sidles up to Eigg's main jetty where a human chain of passengers and locals quickly forms to pull about a ton of camping equipment up from the hold and stash it onto a waiting tractor trailer.

"You're only here for three bloody days!" moans Ronnie the captain as the rucksacks keep streaming from boat to shore. When a pre-packed bag of kindling is passed along the line, the quayside echoes with snorts of derision from the locals towards their largely metropolitan guests.

The locals actually turn out to be lovely and not at all the bunch of weather-hardened cynics they might appear on first view. Less than a hundred of them live on the entire island yet they welcome this friendly invasion with both curiosity and excitement. And it's an invasion that's untested – this is the first ever Away Game, a spin-off of the Fence Collective's annual Home Game gathering held in their seaside home town of Anstruther over on Scotland's east coast.

The collective was founded in the mid-to-late 1990s by local musician Kenny Anderson to provide an umbrella for like-minded, independently inclined musicians, many of whom, like Kenny, wore beards and carried acoustic guitars. More familiarly known by his performing name of King Creosote, he retains the role of spiritual leader of this raggle-taggle brigade. Several of them share his preference for unconventional stage aliases. Among their ranks are solo performers who've jettisoned their birth

THIS MUST BE THE PLACE

names and instead answer to monikers like The Pictish Trail, Lone Pigeon and HMS Ginafore.

Fence's innate independence is matched by the independence of the islanders. They're a good fit. The Isle of Eigg Heritage Trust owns the island and there are pretty much no laws here, thus no police presence. To plenty, this will instantly bring to mind Edward Woodward's police sergeant in *The Wicker Man*, dispatched from the mainland to investigate the disappearance of a young girl on the apparently lawless island of Summerisle, but who winds up feeling the heat of a ritual pyre.

Johnny Lynch – the Fence Collective's second-in-command and this weekend's main organiser – fended off any concerns about such an event being repeated when he posted his Away Game survival guide online. "Will I get burnt to death in a giant effigy of a man woven from wicker?" went one of the questions. "No. Eigg's sea name is Isle of the Big Women, so most probably it will be an effigy of a woman with giant boobies."

Some might wish the emergency services were actually a little closer to hand. On that first hike to the bumpy field that's doubling as the weekend's campsite, we come across a Transit van in a spot of bother. Traffic on Eigg is almost non-existent, the roads empty. (Although, as in an ongoing gag in another film set on the west coast, Bill Forsyth's *Local Hero*, a quad bike seems to zip past at an impossible speed on the hour every hour.)

Yet this van has contrived to place one of its back wheels over the edge of a cliff. A modest cliff, I grant you, but a cliff nonetheless. A tractor soon appears to shunt it back to safety, albeit to the detriment of the Transit's rear lights. The van belongs to Fence's local bakery, invited over from

Fife to handle some of the festival's catering duties. It later transpires that the cargo in danger of disappearing over the cliff edge wasn't their trademark spinach-and-ricotta rolls but something more precious – Johnny Flynn, the celebrated young folk singer and one of Saturday night's star turns (and, fact fans, half-brother to Jerome Flynn of 'Robson &...' fame).

The islanders have thrown themselves into this festival. When they've not been utilising their tractors to form an ad hoc fourth emergency service, they've been rather busy – building stages out of pallets, digging giant holes for the compost toilets, making industrial quantities of lasagne to feed the artists...

It seems that the live music scene – a landscape of ticket scalpers, overpriced drinks and inexplicable booking fees – still contains pockets of well-meaning folk. The voluntary spirit of my old university Ents crew appears to be alive and well and living in the picturesque locale of the Inner Hebrides. And knowing that a generosity of spirit is underpinning this weekend's gathering, that there's no faceless promoter getting unfeasibly rich off the back of it, makes the music sound even better.

Ah, yes, the music. Tent erected – not an easy task if you 1) are a technical buffoon; 2) are under darkening skies with a firm breeze at your back; and 3) are still visibly wobbly from seasickness – it's time for the weekend to really start. The two stages sit up the hill from the harbour, hidden in woodland and thus offering the perfect backdrop for some earthy folk music.

Not that the Away Game is populated exclusively by guitar-strumming troubadours. Sure, there are plenty of these, but Fence is a broad church, its open doors welcoming a diverse congregation. Over the next two days and nights, among many others we'll hear the wide-screen rock of British Sea Power, Brian Eno collaborator Jon Hopkins' headspinning electronica, and the full-on ceilidh experience of Daimh.

As well as being emcee on both stages, Johnny Lynch will perform both electro-folk as the solo Pictish Trail and high-energy techno-pop as one half of Silver Columns. There's even room on the bill for Eigg's token metal band, Massacre Cave. They take their name from the location of a particularly gruesome episode of 16th-century clan warfare that saw the island's entire population of nearly 400 rounded up and suffocated to death in one of its caves. I'm guessing that it would be in poor taste to request a cover of Iron Maiden's *Bring Your Daughter To The Slaughter*.

No massacres this weekend, though – hurrah! Just hours and hours of lovely, lovely music, enthusiastically received by a couple of hundred super-friendly people, increasingly uninhibited by alcohol. The performances alternate between Eigg's wooden ceilidh hall – usually home to, so the islanders boast, the best ceilidhs here in the Small Isles, the archipelago that includes the equally cutely named Rum and Muck – and a marquee set up round the back on the grassy floor of the island's sole tennis court.

I don't think I've ever watched music in a more beautiful setting. Colorado has the Red Rocks Amphitheatre and California boasts the Hollywood Bowl, but for me this scene easily trumps those. The ceilidh hall's outer walls wear a necklace of twinkling fairy lights, while a campfire crackles healthily a few yards away. High above the woods, the towering outline of An Sgurr, Eigg's highest point, dissolves as dusk moves to dark, blue into black.

Nature's not the only restorative force. Never doubt the power of live performance to distract and heal someone still fragile from an extended bout of vomiting. Stepping over the threshold of the ceilidh hall, I'm immediately enveloped by the music of the one-man act known as Withered Hand. His songs are sung in a high, almost-broken voice that sounds just like Neil Young would if he were a hairy young man from Edinburgh called Dan (which is exactly who Withered Hand is). His music is the perfect welcome to the weekend. A can of stomach-steadying Guinness in either hand, I perch on a window sill and let the songs cover me like a warming, chunky cardigan. I'm feeling human again. Normal.

In fact, I'm feeling much better than normal. I gaze around the room. We all seem to be experiencing the same thing. We might be a long way from where we all started out this morning (in addition to that boat ride, Eigg is a five-hour train journey north of Glasgow), but this wooden hut feels like the scene of some kind of homecoming, even though I barely know a soul here. Jane and the boys are more than 500 miles away, but there's a strong sense of fraternity and fellowship here among the all-in-it-together woodland folk. We belong together.

It's not just a matter of geography. We're also a long way from the usual festival experience. There's no security team blocking our path, no fencing separating us from areas upon which we must not trespass. Not a high-visibility tabard in sight.

"Our audiences have become our friends," Kenny Anderson will explain to me the following day when we take a stroll through the woods and up into the foothills of An Sgurr. "It's like a recurring wedding event. People who sell hundreds of thousands never have this connection. When it gets to 12,000 in a field, what chance have you got then? None, because you're relying on third, fourth and fifth parties. If your security are arseholes, you look like arseholes." And this intimacy extends to the artists. "We rely on the bands we do invite being music fans themselves. We want them to be part of it. There's no hierarchy."

Accordingly, the usual lines drawn between performer and punter are not just blurred, they're invisible. Off stage, the musicians become the audience. Even if they wanted to remain aloof, there are no dressing rooms to skulk away to. There's nowhere to hide. We're all in it together.

Perhaps the bar staff have slipped a dram into my Guinness, but I can't help getting ridiculously caught up in the magic of the occasion. There's something very special about seeing someone play who's little more than an arm's length away. It's a world away from the larger festivals where the big screen confirms that the faraway insects on the faraway stage are indeed your musical heroes whom you've shelved out serious money to see in the flesh. Why pay to simply watch TV in a field while being pushed and jostled? My experience of watching Gorillaz in that scrum at Glastonbury comes to mind.

It's the polar opposite here; people budge up to make space for you on the floor or bench or window sill. Yet both experiences come under the banner of 'festival'. As Friday night deepens, things get fuzzier and more energetic. I move on to the spirits and even find myself displaying some inept dancing during the sets of both Silver Columns and Jon Hopkins.

It's 3am when I stumble back down the moonlit lane and across rock-strewn streams to the campsite. The last time I was up at this hour (it was only last week, to be honest), I was trying to usher a wide-awake toddler back to sleep. But now it's me who needs the kip and I'm rather pleased, despite the best efforts of a stiff north-westerly, to find my tent exactly where I left it.

Saturday is equally as magical as Friday. We start off in the ceilidh hall with a hangover-clearing set from a black-humoured young Welshman known as Sweet Baboo. He becomes an instant hit with me, a splendidly bumbling charmer, never more bumbling or charming than when he gleefully tells the story of how the Wales Tourist Board paid good money to use his tune *How I'd Live My Life* in their TV advertising, despite it being about "how Cardiff is a shithole".

From there we cross to the marquee to be entertained by another one-man band eschewing his birth name, Player Piano. This American – real name Jeremy – seems to be the person with the most painful hangover in the whole tent, his state of inertia and confusion compounded when his sister calls him from Indiana halfway through his set.

The weather's beautiful today and I really fancy taking an hour or two out to scale the heights of An Sgurr, but the music won't let me. There's simply too much good stuff on offer. In particular, I want to catch Cate Le Bon (dark folk, Carmarthenshire's answer to Nico), Kid Canaveral (neat indie-pop) and Rozi Plain (delicate acoustic gems). In their own different ways, each puts in a compelling performance. But those are just the performers whose music I'm already familiar with. There's plenty on the bill I'm a stranger to – Fence stalwarts like Come On Gang!

and Gummi Bako. Slow Club, in particular, are rated by several of my pals. My sense of musical curiosity, blunted by writing about records and bands in order to pay the bills, seems to be resharpening itself.

I'm getting lost in the music. When I'm commissioned to review gigs, they're something I have to gaze upon from the fringes, the semi-detached observer. What's getting my groove back here on Eigg, the reason I'm falling back in love again, is that the burden of duty has been lifted. Yes, I am here on assignment for *The Sunday Times*, but they only want an impressionistic report covering the whole weekend. I don't have to study each and every perform-ance in forensic detail, second-guessing the song titles.

Accordingly, I'm freed up, untied. Able to give myself up to the moment. Able to be swallowed up by the music being played right in front of my nose. It's a familiar taste from times past. I'm back to being a punter, a fan.

Afternoon unwinds into evening and, as with every event that Fence hosts, the bar is doing a roaring trade. Indeed, you suspect that the usual gross domestic product of the island is being eclipsed in a single weekend. But, despite the enthusiastic drinking and the fact that the ceilidh hall has just two people behind the bar, they manage something that almost every other music venue can't: we all get served extraordinarily quickly and with plenty of good humour.

In fact, the only place where a queue can be found is at the bakers' stall, where their legendary stovies, a Scottish hot meat-and-potato stew, are selling like, er, hot meat-and-potato stews. (Good job they're here, too. The harbourside café closed early because it ran out of food. But don't you worry about me. I won't fade away.

I'm not one to go camping without an emergency supply of Cheddars. The breakfast of champions. The lunch and dinner of champions, too.)

Queues are in short supply and so too are the usual festival mark-ups that take advantage of a captive audience. The only place where a scam is occurring is on the pathway between the two stages where the local kids are taking advantage of the passing human traffic. They might live on an isolated island but these kids' entrepreneurial spirit and grasp of economics are sharp. Think *Lord of the Flies* meets *The Apprentice*. They've devised their own fairground attraction – Can Golf. It's a simple game: the competitor stands on a wobbly, five-foot-high pile of wooden pallets and, using a stick, tries to hit flattened drink cans into a small area marked out by a coil of leftover plastic piping. They're doing swift business.

I have a go, tipsily scrambling on top of the pallets with at least half of my dignity still intact. Of my allotted five cans, I manage to successfully hit two into the designated area. But my prize isn't great. Just two jellybeans, for which I've paid a pound. But before a disgruntled missive can be fired off to Trading Standards, the enterprise abruptly shuts up shop. One of the 'golfers', whose state of advanced refreshment means he'd have enough difficulty standing upright on terra firma let alone on this unsteady stack of pallets, takes a swing at a can, falls off the pile and squashes one of the children. Game over.

Just as the golf tournament ends, Kenny Anderson – as King Creosote – is striking up his band. And, from the opening chords, it's clear he's playing to the converted. Later on, we enjoy tremendous sets from a firing British Sea Power, Johnny Flynn and his absorbing semi-Gothic tales, and a joyfully wonky Pictish Trail. But it's Kenny who provides the defining moment of the weekend. When he slips into his song *Not One Bit Ashamed*, everyone in the marquee joins in on a chorus that can only be described as anthemic, chanting with all the passion of a partisan football crowd.

My skin prickles and my heart pounds. I'm also beaming from ear to ear, in a way I probably never have in recent years – at least not outside the maternity unit. As a measure of the abundant fraternity being felt on this small, faraway Hebridean island, this communal singalong can't be beaten. You can almost hear the purring, approving tones of Alan Hansen. "The Fence lads have a magnificent unbeaten home record, but could they do the business on the road? On the evidence of this, they travel well. The Away Game has been a terrific away victory. Three points in the bag. Outstanding."

Kenny, anxious beforehand despite his ever-present smiles, sighs with relief. "Had this first Away Game not been magical in some way, we'd have blown it. The fact that it had to be good seems to have made it good." During his set, he explains to a packed marquee how pleasing it's been both to be reacquainted with old friends and to meet new ones, including some mysterious bloke called The Whitey Guy. Well, not that mysterious. Yesterday evening I was chewing the cud with Kenny when, out of the darkness, an accusatory finger was thrust in my face.

"It's you! You're the fucking Whitey Guy!"

The accuser, despite clearly having taken a few stout measures of drink, had made a correct identification.

"You're the guy on the boat. I've never seen someone look so ill in my life!"

For the next couple of hours, anyone and everyone who was within earshot of Kenny was introduced to me, The Whitey Guy, the lily-livered land-lubber who turned the whitest shade of pale.

At least I think that was last night. Time has lost its relevance this weekend. When The Pictish Trail finishes his Saturday night set at three on Sunday morning, the schedule's running two and a half hours late. There are still five bands to go on. No-one's bothered, though. Well, save for a few of us responsible souls who diligently retreat into our sleeping bags at 4am. We've got a ferry to catch in the morning, after all.

The remainder opt to party right through as night bleeds into day. Later that afternoon, they cram onto a tractor trailer for a bumpy ride up to a beach at the northern end of the island, the beautifully named Singing Sands. While they're there, the ceilidh tradition of sacrificially burning the stage is upheld, before a handful of musicians play around the resulting fire.

I'd love to have stayed, but I've still got a full 25 hours of travelling before I see Jane and the kids again. Boat, train, bus, plane and car are all ahead of me before I need to do the school run tomorrow afternoon. I should just about make it.

The first of those 25 hours involves stepping back onboard the *Sheerwater*. Bearing in mind his underplaying of conditions on the way out, I head straight to Ronnie the captain for the latest.

"Calm as a millpond," he deadpans. I take that to mean "relentlessly undulating but not quite as bad as the outward journey" and prepare myself accordingly. As it happens, Ronnie's completely correct. It's a pancake-flat ride back to the mainland, one that allows me to actually converse with my fellow passengers without the need for a carrier bag to be glued to my mouth.

We compare the weather conditions of the voyage out and this voyage back. It turns out I'm talking to the one other guy who was sick on the way over. "I'm Stu the Spew." "I'm The Whitey Guy." "You're The Whitey Guy? Kenny played a song for you last night!" In the tiny corner of the music industry occupied by the Fence Collective, I appeared to have passed into some sort of marginally legendary status. I lean back to bask in the golden light currently beaming down onto the open deck, mulling over what's surely been my best-ever festival experience. Eigg sadly gets smaller and smaller in the distance.

But then Ronnie cuts the engine, just as he did several times on the way over. What now? Some kind of one-off tsunami heading our way, ready to toss us into dark, wet oblivion? Not at all. As if the last two days haven't been magical enough, a minke whale rises magnificently from the water and escorts us back to port. V Festival could never give you that.

❧   ❧   ❧   ❧   ❧

A small Hebridean island isn't the only unlikely venue for a reputable music festival. Some are even stranger.

Gazing down from the wall, cheesy grins to the fore, are autographed portraits of overenthusiastic fitness fanatic Mr Motivator and the not-at-all-fanatical-about-fitness darts giant Cliff Lazarenko. To my left is a garishly coloured, four-storey indoor soft-play centre; beyond it, some curious structure called Puppet Castle. And in front of me, five young men from Florida, collectively answering to the name Surfer Blood, are doing their darnedest to make my ears bleed via the medium of extremely loud electric guitars.

This odd coupling of family-friendly leisure pursuits and imported indie rock can only mean one thing – we're at Butlin's in Minehead, on the blustery Somerset coast, for the tribal gathering known as All Tomorrow's Parties. This is where, on three or four weekends a year, the indie set comes to play, a three-day blast of lager, fairground attractions and cooler-than-thou musical turns.

The event's origins lie in a festival called Bowlie, dreamed up by the fey indie collective Belle & Sebastian, that debuted at Pontins in Camber Sands on the Sussex coast in 1999. You suspect it was an idea that had been in gestation ever since the band's frontman Stuart Murdoch worked at Butlin's when he was young. Renamed and re-located, it's become one of the most innovative and keenly awaited fixtures on the festival circuit calendar.

I'm kind of embarrassed that it's taken me ten years to show my face around here. I live in the same county, just a leisurely hour or so's drive away. It's a hell of a lot easier to get to than Eigg. But, finally, this weekend I'm losing my ATP cherry.

I've been to Butlin's Minehead before, though. We brought the kids here last year for a short break. Indeed, the last act I saw up on the very stage where Surfer Blood are now playing was an undeniably impressive unicycle display team.

It might be snobbish to admit that there was more than a slight sense of embarrassment that we'd chosen to bring the kids here. I'm not sure we mentioned it to our friends from the ante-natal group for fear of social ostracism. I was even more unsure about this weekend. Indie's snobbery levels can be set quite high. Mine too. And a location still haunted by the ghosts of Ted Bovis, Jeffrey Fairbrother and Gladys Pugh isn't the most obvious for an über-cool clientele. I should be running a mile.

But there are no knobbly-knees competitions happening today. No donkey derbies. No old blokes flopped in deck-chairs with hankies on their heads to keep their brains from baking.

I needn't have worried a jot. Within just a few minutes on-site, it's clear that hosting a music festival here is a simple yet brilliant idea that I've been wrong to avoid all this time. Such snobbery, such squeamishness, was woefully misplaced. Not only does ATP erase all preconceptions, it also – rather effortlessly – outscores most other festivals.

Its virtues are plentiful. A roof over your head, in the form of a plain but functional chalet. A proper bed with clean sheets. Toilets with loo roll. Toilets that flush. Umpteen on-site bars. Late-closing grocery stores. The opportunity to self-cater using a proper cooker. A curry buffet. An on-site Pizza Hut. Jellybean dispensers on every corner (and offering more generous rations than the children of Eigg). Go-karts. Full-size snooker tables. Walls and walls of arcade machines... What else could you either want or need? Mud? Waterlogged tents? Seeing your favourite band from a distance of several hundred yards? Thought not.

The comfort levels also extend to numbers. It's a full house of 6,000 this weekend. A modest capacity when it comes to festivals but, as with the Away Game, ATP knows its constituency, knows what that constituency wants and shrugs off any pressure to increase numbers by moving elsewhere. A lid has been kept on things.

The man in charge of that lid is Barry Hogan. He's been involved since Belle & Sebastian first hit upon the original concept and, when the Glaswegians withdrew from the project after that first event, Barry took the baton and ran. Following a quick renaming ceremony, for more than a decade now he's been successfully convincing the sometimes-sneery indie constituency that a seaside holiday camp is absolutely the right crucible for a festival.

"It's fair to say that a lot of people wouldn't be seen dead in Butlins or Pontins normally," he explains when I track him down scurrying between stages. I agree. Were *Hi-De-Hi* still on our TV sets, he'd have no chance of filling the chalets. The distance of a couple of decades means that irony can be employed to circumnavigate any social embarrassment.

"It's such a great location. And it's not in a field. The idea of sharing a toilet with 50,000 crusties is not my idea of fun. We at ATP like to have showers and stuff. We're designed for a more civilised audience full of more discerning music fans who like checking out all the bands rather than wearing a silly hat and dancing in a field to Jamiroquai."

The combination of relative domestic comfort and unusual surroundings is a core element of ATP's identity; another is inviting a special guest to curate the weekend.

"I felt having a curator was a great concept," explains Barry. "It was like having one of your favourite bands making a mixtape, but for the stage." Among those appointed to the role over the years have been Portishead,

My Bloody Valentine, the actor Vincent Gallo and the art world's brotherly *enfants terribles* Jake and Dinos Chapman.

But surely, by appointing a curator, Barry has abdicated the best bit of running a festival. Isn't most of the fun picking the star turns? Why leave yourself the unglamorous tasks of logistics and contracts and visas?

"One of the reasons that ATP's lasted so long is that it's different people's interpretations of mixtapes," he sagely notes. Ah, a neat application of business logic. The name and the location might remain the same, but the artistic content can vary widely from curator to curator. The event thus finds itself in a not-unattractive state of constant renewal.

If a curator has sufficient currency and cachet, his/her/their appointment alone can sell all 6,000 tickets before a single act is announced. Just as this weekend has. Choosing the roster are Pavement, the doyens of American indie who, as well as playing live themselves for the first time in the UK in over a decade, have largely filled the bill with guitar-toting compatriots with a similar taste in – what they'd call – sneakers.

Pavement's relative conservatism is a tad disappointing, especially bearing in mind the sense of adventure shown by the previous ATP curator – *Simpsons* creator Matt Groening. He put together a variety show that found room for, among others, wailing hippy harpists from California (Joanna Newsom), avant-garde art collectives (The Residents) and West African rhythm-and-blues practitioners (Amadou & Mariam).

Not that curators have absolute carte blanche to dictate artistic matters. Even when the event sells out quickly and there's no longer a commercial pressure to answer to, caution is still applied. It's not a licence to indulge yourself.

"You can get more experimental when it's sold out, but we still don't want to alienate people. 'We've got our money now. Let's put on a shit line-up.' It's got to be something that people walk away from thinking 'Wow, that was great. I want to come back.'"

Barry's level-headed, long-game approach can't be argued with. I let him get back to chivvying the bands along and head out into the night air, casting myself, like plenty of others this weekend, I'm sure, in the role of curator, dreaming up my ultimate ATP line-up.

My brain's a whirl, calculating how well The Skatalites would carry the main stage in the cavernous Pavilion and salivating at the prospect of a solo Ry Cooder holding court in the more intimate Reds bar. This latter venue proudly declares itself the "home of the Redcoats". Thankfully they appear to have been given the weekend off.

Aimlessly wandering across the site, I can't help but notice that the rows and rows of chalets do still have something of the army camp about them. This is despite the best efforts of Butlins' marketeers who've given each cluster of chalets and each avenue a wildly optimistic, aspirational name. I've just passed through the quarter known as Pacific Wharf on my way to Atlantic Bay. On the way back, I might take a stroll along Flamingo Grove. Sounds nice. Tropical, even.

The architecture notwithstanding, this is a far from unpleasant evening amble. It's approaching 10pm and several of the big names are currently on stage, but the accommodation blocks are surprisingly busy and buzzing, resonating with the low murmur of TV sets and the sound of supper being taken. Those at home don't seem to feel the pressure of catching each and every performance this weekend. Or, more likely, they're simply pacing themselves wisely, warming up with an episode of *QI* before heading out of their chalets to see in the wee small hours, bouncing between stages, culminating in a DJ set from Smiths drummer Mike Joyce some time close to sunrise.

Certainly there are plenty of distractions to draw you away from the music. I get sidelined myself this weekend, taking an hour or two out in the Hotshots sports bar to catch up with Australia and Pakistan battling it out in the World Twenty20 cricket semi-final. A few others have the same idea and we form an ad hoc panel of would-be pundits, glued to proceedings on the big screen. The delights of alt-country collective Calexico, playing barely 70 feet away on the other side of a bank of grabber machines, go wanting.

The next afternoon, one of those cricket-watchers – Shaun, a graphic designer from Bournemouth – misses yet more music, this time inadvertently. So engrossed is he in an impromptu air hockey tournament in the amusement arcade that he clean forgets to catch one of his heroes – American Music Club frontman Mark Eitzel. "Bugger" is his economic summation of events when he realises that just five minutes remain of Eitzel's set. (Incidentally, Shaun's not alone in succumbing to the allure of air hockey. Based on wholly unscientific observations this weekend, it's clearly the fairground attraction of choice for the discerning indie hipster.)

But, unlike Shaun, most of ATP's punters are paying attention to the musical offerings – very close attention, in fact. These are the indie cognoscenti, those who know how to choose between Wax Fang in the Pavilion and The 3Ds upstairs on Centre Stage. Not that musical discoveries aren't being made, though. Julie and Jon, a pair of students who've made the shortish haul over from Bath, have trusted Jon's love of this weekend's curators to deliver a good line-up. "If it's good enough for Pavement," Jon declares of the bill, "it's good enough for me. I guess it's like having a sneaky peak at their record collections or their iPods. And who wouldn't want to do that?"

So far, the couple have been awakened to plenty of new sounds and seem particularly taken with the Californian teen band Avi Buffalo. "He's a seriously talented guy," says Julie of the band's leader. A guitarist herself, she's clearly thrilled – and perhaps a little bit depressed – by how annoyingly precocious this 19-year-old is. "He's two years younger than me. And about 20 times better."

Avi Buffalo have made an impression on me too. These youngsters have the daunting task of being the weekend's first band, taking to the stage on Friday afternoon when many punters are still either negotiating the windy Somerset lanes, relieving the local Tesco of its stocks of instant noodles, cider and paracetamol, or drawing lots to determine who's going to have which bedroom in the shared chalet.

No matter. The band are both visibly and audibly delighted to be here at this provincial holiday camp in a faraway corner of the UK – "ATP rocks!" whoops one of them. It's a sentiment shared by many of their fellow countrymen this weekend, several of whom regularly remind us how "stoked" they are to be playing. Indeed, Surfer Blood's bass player rather sweetly sums up the significance of the occasion to them. "Did you ever witness the pinnacle of a career before?" is the rhetorical question posed to a couple of thousand punters.

Make no bones about it, ATP is an inspired idea, brilliantly executed and, through the guest curator system, continually refreshed. Just like the Away Game, this is no perfunctory bash that simply goes through the motions with its eye almost exclusively on its financial bottom line. It's an event that takes care, not advantage, of its loyal constituency – that combination of homegrown indie kids and overseas enthusiasts, air hockey converts and part-time cricket fans. For all, it's a 72-hour daze of enjoyment and escapism. Just as Billy Butlin would have wanted it. And I rap myself on the knuckles for being so snooty.

Well after the last band has unplugged their amps for the night, there are still pockets of fun and frivolity around the site, whether it's DJ sets that won't let up this side of dawn or impromptu chalet gatherings fuelled by those supplies of cider and instant noodles. Never mind tomorrow – for now it's about all tonight's parties.

For some, anyway. I coax the Honda into life, bump over the level crossing and head for home. I need to take Finn to his swimming lesson in a few hours. Back to life, back to reality.

The hour is stupidly late but I feel remarkably energised. Fired up, even. Not by this weekend's bill, artistically narrow by ATP standards, but by its winning formula. In fact, I'm so enamoured with the concept that, when Monday comes around, I'm back in the car and charging across three counties for a meeting at the WOMAD festival offices. (And charge I do. I'm so energised that I get a speeding ticket en route.)

There I make an impassioned case for them to hold their own out-of-season bash right there at Butlin's Minehead. It'd be perfect. There's even a neatly alliterative name just waiting to be used – Winter WOMAD.

Obviously I've got my eye on the curator's chair. We'll have no special guests choosing the bands round here. The concept is a no-brainer, I'm sure of it. A slam-dunk, a shoo-in. But maybe there's something wrong with their phone system. Why else would I not have had the call yet…?

8

EVERYBODY KNOWS THIS IS NOWHERE

Destination: Motorpoint Arena Cardiff
Occasion: Elbow enormodome show
Miles travelled so far: 3,353
Fellow concert-goers: 7,499
Guided tours of tour buses: 3
Three-course backstage banquets consumed: 1
£4 bottles of lager bought: 0

Let me take you by the hand and lead you to the summer of 1987. Four carefree teenagers – their A-level exam papers still on the desks of the official markers, yet to be issued with the chronically underachieving grades that will sentence them to a year of revision and resits – are zipping along a dual carriageway. The sun is bright, the sky is blue and this year's totem album, U2's *The Joshua Tree*, is blasting out of all four car windows. A record that emphasises the band's growing fascination with the USA, its primary purpose is clearly to provide the soundtrack to a thousand road trips along the deserted highways of Arizona. We're having to make do with the A34.

The tape's now on its third play. As the bass and drums come crashing in again on *Where The Streets Have No Name*, we're egging our designated driver to put a little more pressure on the accelerator, keen to see the speedometer needle graze the 100mph mark. It does. We cheer. Carefree, careless and immortal. Fun, fun, fun 'til Daddy takes the Ford Sierra away.

The Joshua Tree is on the stereo because we're on our way to Birmingham, specifically the NEC, to see U2 live, in the flesh. This is, let's remind ourselves, only the second gig I've been to. And last time I was right under the singer's nose, with the set-list as a souvenir. I'm fully expecting this to be equally special and am brimming over with excitement and euphoria. Kid in a sweet shop.

That excitement and euphoria is slightly muted when we arrive in a car park the size of my home town. It takes the best part of ten minutes to walk from car to main entrance. On the way, I spy a poster for next week's hottest ticket, the annual trade expo of the British flooring industry. I imagine such an event would need some serious square yardage and, yes, when we shamble inside, the vast space reveals itself. This place is frigging huge. Capital letters HUGE. And our tickets deposit us far, far from the stage. Those roadies, that drum kit, those guitars… they're in a different postal district.

I'm trying not to sink the buoyant mood of the party, but it's difficult to suppress a deep sigh. Even with my severely limited gigging experience, I realise that trying to pick out some matchstick men from a distance of around

200 yards isn't the best way to experience a live spectacle. And when the main act come on stage, Bono – far from the tallest man on the planet, even if the ego suggests otherwise – looks minuscule. A Playmobil figure with a god complex.

I can see the back of the auditorium much more clearly than the stage. Mainly because it's just two rows behind me. Row ZZZ, I presume. Before me, almost 16,000 others have better, closer views of Dublin's most famous musical sons. I'm not the world's most dedicated U2 fan, but I was still open to submerging myself in the music, to losing myself. Perhaps even a slight out-of-body experience during that semi-orchestral bit halfway through *The Unforgettable Fire*. Instead, I just find myself gazing around the audience. Distanced and dislocated.

Despite my tender years and unfocused teenage brain, one thing rings loud and true. And it's rung loud and true ever since. Why is the success of a band measured by how small they look from the cheap seats? It defies logic. The more popular the band, the bigger the venue. The bigger the venue, the worse the view. And, of course, the more expensive the ticket.

People just accept this orthodoxy, many thousands squinting the evening away in arenas on any given night of the week. But since that depressing night during the summer of '87, I've kept my distance, electing not to set foot over the threshold of one of those ridiculous hangars. Now, though, having thought U2 had successfully scared me off for life, I'm renouncing – for the sake of research, admittedly – my faith. A quarter of a century later, I'm going back in.

This time, my destination is Cardiff, not Birmingham, and I'm now travelling alone. No car full of speed-freak teenagers. No carefree fatalism. No wind in my hair (if only). The pace is more sedate. The volume on the car stereo is still turned up, but the forty-something's listening pleasure is different from the teenager's. The afternoon play is about to start on Radio 4. And it's on loud because the car's making its trademark cacophony of unhealthy noises that I really should get a mechanic to cure.

I'm off to rub shoulders – and possibly even hang out – with Elbow, the Bury band whose rise, having scooped the Mercury Prize in 2008, has been phenomenal. They've gone from neglected cult heroes to being the kind of band whose music accompanies the slo-mo montage at the end of every TV sporting occasion of note. Recently anointed as bona fide household names, they're currently on their first full arena tour. Tonight, their charabanc stops over in South Wales.

Unlike many enormodomes, Cardiff International Arena – or the Motorpoint Arena Cardiff as it's been rebadged, having sold its naming rights for a reported seven-figure fee to "the UK's leading car supermarket" – is right in the centre of town. At a normal-sized, common-or-garden gig, mid-afternoon would still be early doors for someone to arrive to observe the backstage preparations. But I'm more than a little late to catch the action. Arena shows occupy a different time zone. By this point in the day, much of the work is complete, many of the crew having already put in nine or ten hours of service. The heavy lifting's done, at least; now it's all about fine-tuning the light and sound or artistically arranging the merchandise display.

The crew got here somewhat earlier than I did – although, in my defence, they didn't have to do the school run this morning. They're early risers, these roadies. Barely three hours after the last truck belonging to yesterday's performers McFly headed away from the venue and off into the Cardiff night, Elbow's wagons rolled into town, ready to discharge their cargo as soon as the clock struck 5.30am, an hour only otherwise kept by office cleaners, milkmen and urban foxes.

Having got the nod from the man at the security gate, I cross the loading bay, weaving my way around articulated trucks and tour buses, and striding across great spaghetti pools of cables. It's just like being back in the BBC compound at Glastonbury, but thankfully without the eye-tearing stench of those latrines. There's no sense of rush or panic round here. Calm and controlled. Tonight's support, the Dublin outfit Villagers, idly kick a ball around the loading bay.

I wander along the corridors backstage, following the makeshift signs to the stage. The walls are lined with photographs of the greats who've trod the Cardiff International boards on nights past. Whether intended or not, these photos are the equivalent of the passive-aggressive 'This Is Anfield' sign that both welcomes and intimidates Liverpool's opponents as they emerge from the tunnel into the furnace of 45,000 screaming Scousers. But, while the action shots of genuine legends like The Four Tops and BB King might make an act feel somewhat insecure about its own place in music history as it nervously approaches the stage, I can't help thinking the framed photo of earnest but wafer-thin popsters Deacon Blue surely has the opposite effect.

As I get closer to the hall itself, I become aware of an enormous flock of flight cases either side of me. A *really* enormous flock of flight cases. Not a couple of dozen, but scores and scores. Hundreds, even. I keep walking and reach the wings. Loads more of them are parked up at the side of the stage, as well as underneath it. I start to count them. It rapidly becomes apparent that this is a futile exercise. I get as far as 170 before getting bored. There's at least the same amount again in my eye line. I'm beginning to get a sense of the scale of the whole operation.

I gaze around at this vast, empty shell. Cardiff's is by no means one of the UK's biggest arenas (the O2 in Greenwich and Manchester's MEN Arena can both hold nearly three times as many people), but you could still comfortably park a couple of 747s inside here. It's a huge cattle shed, pretty much devoid of character, of history, of a sense of place. Give me a venue with its own identity any day. The pleasing Victoriana of former music hall Hackney Empire, perhaps. Or the atmosphere of a deconsecrated church, like Islington's Union Chapel or St George's in Bristol. Even if it's a dingy back room of a pub, there'll still be plenty about it to distinguish it from every other dingy pub back room. Here, the sign might say Cardiff, but I could be anywhere. Or, indeed, nowhere.

And while we're having a moan, why on earth would a venue surrender its one true identity – its name – for the fat cheque of the sponsor? They clearly haven't learned from the Marathon/Snickers and Mr Dog/Cesar debacles that came before it. Why cast aside the reputable name (here I guess I should reluctantly use the word 'brand') that's been built up over years, even decades, and start all over again?

I'm also very sceptical about its worth for the bene-
factor. They surely can't recoup their seven-figure spend.
Who, among the thousands standing in the Motorpoint
Arena Cardiff later this evening, will instantly consider
the purchase of a new set of wheels simply because
a car dealership's name is above the door? And does
anyone in Cardiff actually refer to the place by its new
moniker, anyhow? Almost all still know it as the Cardiff
International Arena – and they pretty much all refer to it
by its CIA acronym.

It's the same all over. No self-respecting Newcastle
United fan could ever remotely consider referring to St
James' Park as the Sports Direct Arena. Similarly, to
the hopelessly devoted music fan of a certain vintage –
and no matter what's printed on the ticket – the HMV
Apollo will always be the Hammersmith Odeon, while
the Carling Reading Weekender will never be known as
anything other than Reading Festival.

Whether carrying the name of a sponsor or not,
anonymous arenas are all that the hardened roadie,
working for some of the world's top acts, will see. Robin
is one such person, although to call him a mere roadie
would be insulting, like referring to the Governor of
the Bank of England as some bloke who spends his
day counting money. Robin's the production manager
for this entire tour, the man upon whose shoulders the
whole shebang balances. But despite this Herculean
burden, he's cucumber-cool, thanks to his vast experience on endless tours with the likes of Amy Winehouse,
Florence & The Machine, Snow Patrol and Kaiser
Chiefs. His burden doesn't wobble an inch. Shoulders
steady, brow unfevered.

"I'm well aware of my responsibilities," his soft Scottish voice confirms. "Thousands of people have each paid £35 or so for their Friday night out. And that Friday night out depends on me making sure everything happens on time." Not that the hundreds of shows he's overseen have left him jaded or bitter, unable to feel the magic any longer. "I still get a bit of a buzz when I'm walking the band to the stage on a sold-out show and the crowd go wild. I'm not embarrassed to admit that."

And it would be perfectly understandable had Robin become jaded and/or bitter. He's spent almost the last decade on tour, away from home for on average around ten months in any calendar year. "I'll have about two weeks at home and start to get bored. I'll get itchy feet and want to go back out again. But I'm hardly home long enough for that to happen. As I come to a finish working with band A, I seem to start working with band B. It keeps it interesting. The 9 to 5 didn't work for me." It seems Robin prefers the 5am to 1am instead, a shift that rather ludicrously "crams three days' work into one".

I let Robin get back to chivvying along the 70-strong crew and – having declined the meat-heavy sandwich selection at Magor Services – realise I'm a little peckish. Back in the labyrinth of backstage corridors, several competing smells are wafting down a stairwell, beckoning me. I follow my nose upstairs to the catering unit.

With my Access All Areas pass stuck to my thigh, I try to pass myself off as one of the local hired help in order to secure a meal. Wisely – and despite having a Welsh wife – I don't try to put on a Cardiff accent. But I'm still far from convincing. Why would a roadie be clutching a notepad and dictaphone, after all? Whether the catering team simply admire my gall or just aren't bothered that there's one more mouth to feed, I get away with it. "Pick a table and the waitress will be over in a minute." Waitress service? Now that is civilised.

When *The Observer*'s review of tonight's show runs a couple of days later, it makes a reference to Guy Garvey resembling "Henry VIII after a particularly heavy supper". Although a little unkind (Guy isn't known to have commissioned the beheading of his nearest and dearest, after all), there's something to this comparison with the most overfed of monarchs. Guy – and the rest of the 70-strong crew – do indeed eat like kings.

The choice of food is exemplary. I expected honest, basic fare, high in carbs to meet the energy demands of a round-the-clock workforce. What I find is a menu that would have even the most jaded Sunday supplement restaurant reviewer salivating like a dog that hasn't had a nibble for a week.

Starters

Tom yum soup
Crispy brie with sweet chilli jam

Mains

Sticky pork chop with sour cream crushed potatoes and jalapeno gravy
Corn-fed chicken fillet with lemon and leek risotto
Teriyaki salmon with oriental greens and udon noodles
Polenta, aubergine and mozzarella stacks with tomato passata
Poached gnocchi with a ricotta and artichoke basil cream

Dessert

*Jamaican gingerbread, poached peaches, mascarpone
and custard
Fruit salad*

And, despite being cooked for 70 people by a tiny catering team in a borrowed kitchen, the food more than lives up to its billing. The proof is in the pudding. And in the starters and mains, too. On this particular element of the arena experience, I've been won over. I should be playing the objective journalist who's charged himself with hunting for the soul of live music but, for now, there's the more pressing matter of mopping up the remains of the ricotta and artichoke basil cream with my last ball of gnocchi.

I take my near-spotless plate back towards the kitchen where I meet Vicky, the woman in charge of keeping the tour watered and fed. Amazingly, there are just four of them achieving this. Vicky details a punishing daily schedule – 17 hours, three meal-times, two hours of supermarket shopping. After serving dinner, they'll be cleaned up and loaded out by around 9pm, just about the time that Elbow take to the stage. "Then we wait for the dressing rooms to empty and clear those. We finish around 12.30, one o'clock. It's a hard graft.

"But it's also a good old life. You get paid for all your days off. If you only do three gigs a week, you still get paid for seven days. And you get to go all over the world and stay in five-star hotels. It's not shabby. I try not to do much more than eight months on tour each year. This is a three-week tour, then next I'm off with Take That for five months. If you do a tour that big, you don't have to work too much for the rest of the year. It depends how much you want to earn. Or how quickly you want to kill yourself. I'd rather lie on a beach..."

I head back to the table where my gingerbread and custard is now waiting for me, steaming. I eavesdrop on my fellow diners. I'm sharing a table with Robin and Tom, the tour manager. They're talking business with two members of the crew, Dave and Johnny, bus driver and truck driver respectively. The four of them are discussing the logistics of a forthcoming European tour and I'm staggered by the extent of the two drivers' knowledge. They seem to have the answer to any question that Tom fires at them about cross-continental travel – the driving times between certain European cities; the times of departures from particular ferry ports; the number of daily flights between Barcelona and Lisbon... It's as if their bonces have been implanted with large portions of Wikipedia, TripAdvisor and the most up-to-date sat nav software.

Twenty minutes later, the fundamentals of getting this travelling circus across Europe and back for a zigzagging series of festival appearances are firmed up. "Without their knowledge," Tom smiles, with undisguised satisfaction, "that would probably have taken my assistant a week to research."

When Robin and Tom head off to further lubricate this already well-oiled operation, Johnny and Dave stay seated. It turns out – quite obviously, if I'd stopped to think about it – they have nothing to do for hours on end. Once they've delivered their respective cargoes, be they the band's instruments or the band themselves, that's it until some time around midnight when those cargoes need shifting on to the next location. So they're definitely up for another cuppa and a chat.

"There's a lot of time when we're sat doing nothing or sat outside hotels just waiting," confirms Dave, who counts Kaiser Chiefs, Belle & Sebastian, The Coral, Mogwai and The Zutons among his clients. "It isn't a glamorous job. It's like an air hostess – glamorous on the outside, but actually just serving teas and coffees. I'm just driving a bus."

But your job is evidently much more exciting and noteworthy than driving the Number 13, half-full with pensioners and their shopping, from town centre to housing estate and back again for eight hours a day.

"Every single person who gets on the bus is just a human being. You don't see them as a rock star. You just see them as a person getting on the bus to go from A to B. After about six months in the job, you stop boasting to friends that you've just had Phil Collins on the bus."

Johnny nods his agreement. "And once that glamour goes, it suddenly dawns on you that if you don't make it to a gig, it's game over. It's a big responsibility. If I was carrying frozen peas on my truck, I wouldn't bat an eyelid about breaking down. But," he declares, with a puff of his chest, "I've never been late for a load-in in 11 years."

Dave owns a fleet of buses and is quick to point out that, although his drivers are kicking their heels during the daytime, the life of a tour bus driver is relentless. They're on the road for around 270 days a year. "We've got buses out now that have been out for three months. And on days off, the drivers don't get a plush hotel like the crew do. They don't go out with everybody and get absolutely slaughtered. They're working. It's the one day they can clean the bus and change the bedding."

Johnny, the self-employed truck driver, butts in. "My day off is spent at Hilton Park Services! And I still have to wee in lay-bys." He catches Dave's eye. "You don't. You've got a toilet!"

The on-board toilets are just one of numerous luxuries. Our tea drained, Dave and I head downstairs to the loading bay where four of his buses are parked up. On the way, he regales me with tales of a life spent ferrying musicians around Europe. He's got a sackful of cracking stories – at least half of which are sadly unpublishable – detailing the personal peccadilloes of rock's high-fliers.

He opens the doors of the band's bus and I quickly realise why he prefers to call them "luxury coaches". There are plush bunks, huge TV screens and games consoles, not to mention fridges the size of walk-in wardrobes, stocked with a selection of refreshments more extensive than that offered by the average corner shop. And, just in case their nightly three-course banquet didn't quite fill the gap, the band's bus even has its own kitchen, ready to satisfy those midnight cravings.

Tour buses equipped to such a high spec might appear a luxury and an indulgence. Just like the capacity of the venue they're playing, the size of a band's transport is a status symbol, a signifier of the stratum they currently occupy. But, as Tom the tour manager later tells me, hiring these high-end vehicles is no extravagant, snoop-cocking exercise. It's actually cost-effective. At a few hundred quid a day all-in – a price that includes bus, driver and fuel – it's eminently cheaper than expensive hotels, transfers and travel. It's more practical too, allowing the management to keep everyone in one place. This way, the bass player isn't left oversleeping in a hotel room in

Antwerp while the rest of the band are halfway down the road to Rotterdam.

And a luxury coach can also double up as a radio studio. Guy Garvey has now slipped aboard Elbow's bus and, behind closed doors and from the comfort of the driver's seat, is recording links for his 6Music show into a DAT machine. It's only when the show is spliced together and broadcast the following Sunday that I realise, while Dave and I were watching him, Guy was watching us. He was telling the nation not only about the activities of the rest of the band, but also about me and Dave enjoying a chinwag in the sunshine. "I'm looking out of the front window. Mark Potter's doing a phone interview, Pete Turner's doing a phone interview and, in a bizarre twist of events, Dave the bus driver is being interviewed by a guy who's talking to all the crew. Even Dave's being interviewed!"

As with the catering, I have to admit that the transport arrangements are impressive. Seductive, even. Whether they're true to the supposedly rough-and-ready soul of live music that I'm hunting down, I'm not convinced. Still, who can deny Elbow a little bit of comfort after 20 years of feeling every bump in the road? Not only have they put in the miles playing every dive from Andover to Aberdeen, but they've also been on what the tabloids would inevitably call "a rollercoaster ride", still bearing the bruises and scars from the way a fickle record industry has manhandled them.

Having subjected Dave the driver to a bunch of my trademark half-witted questions, I now approach Elbow's drummer Richard Jupp to ask him another bunch of half-witted questions. Like how it feels for five old mates from north Manchester to have this whole mini-industry set up around them.

"We've talked about nothing else on this tour – the logistical side of things. It blows our minds that people are giving so much for little old us. We do keep looking at ourselves, thinking 'Five dossers from Bury? All we've done is dick about.' But somehow we've managed to blag our way through. And it's still a blag in our eyes. We look at each other on stage and say 'Fucking hell! Are we here? Are we doing this?' And that's always a really nice moment."

It's certainly a long way from the band's first gig in 1991, in a pub in the Lancashire village of Stubbins, near Ramsbottom. "That place was probably the size that my drum riser is now. We were packed into a corner. Jimmy the landlord, who had a wooden leg, always said to us: 'Don't turn it up past three. And stick to the blues, lads!' Immortal advice. Thankfully we didn't follow it. And now we're here."

But while the band's profile has soared on a near-vertical ascent, the quintet's egos have remained grounded. "Nothing's taken for granted. There's no separation between band and crew. We all eat together, we all have a beer together after the show. I'm more likely to be found outside with the riggers or the drivers – because I can get a bit of gossip out of them!

"Back in the day, outside the Roadhouse or Band On the Wall in Manchester, we used to hand out our flyers, which included a pound off the entry fee. We still say to each other before a sell-out show, 'Have you done your flyers? Have you handed them out?'. Head in the clouds, feet on the ground."

Just then, the production assistant comes to find Richard. I've detained him for so long – although he's been more than happy to talk – that there's a danger of the band not getting on stage on time because they can't find their drummer. Had my waffling detained him any longer, 7,500 impatient Cardiffians would have been looking for my head to impale on a sharp stick.

While Richard dashes off to the dressing room, I saunter into the main hall and gaze around, before heading upstairs to the balcony seats to gain a good vantage point. The most hardcore Elbow fans, those who've been hanging around the front door since mid-afternoon, have got their reward. They're glued to the front barrier – and to the catwalk that extends out into the crowd – like bees around the stickiest honeypot. And they won't budge all night; not 'even' the enticement of a single bottle of Carlsberg for a thoroughly unjustified £4 a pop can persuade them to shift an inch. No surrender, defending their vantage point with all the vigour of Lieutenant Chard's men at Rorke's Drift.

Viewed from the top row of the balcony, the sight of those 7,500 people packed into a single room is, I'm forced to admit, rather impressive. I might not be able to see the whites of their eyes, but I can certainly see the whites of their camera phones. When the band emerge from the shadows of the wings, their passage is captured from all angles by a shower of popping flashbulbs.

And the roar greeting them is what you'd expect, too. Cacophonous and partisan. They slip into the wiry riff of *The Birds*, another swell of cheers rises and the audience is safely in their pocket, exactly where they'll remain for the next two hours. Guy Garvey takes centre stage, the three-piece-suit-wearing tenor, the swift-tongued ringmaster of this travelling circus. It's a role that clearly makes him attractive to a large segment of the women in the audience. When he removes his jacket a few numbers in, wolf-whistles ring out across the hall. "Hardly, but thank you."

Up here on the top tier of the balcony, I concede that it does look something of a spectacle, a proper show. There are some effective light and video touches that certainly enhance the performance without intruding on the music, while the enormous mirrorball that's in place for their song, er, *Mirrorball* is a neat addition. (As stage props go, it's at least infinitely more tasteful than the artistic choices made by AC/DC for their last tour, the centrepiece of which was a 40-foot blow-up doll straddling a full-size steam locomotive.)

To his credit, Guy is certainly reaching out to the room, trying his level best to make this hangar more intimate, more personal. He makes frequent forays into the crowd along his specially constructed catwalk, before putting out a call for a guy in the audience called Adrian Jones. Why so? Has Adrian left the gas on at home? Is his wife being rushed to the local maternity ward where the father-to-be needs to join her immediately? No. Adrian's getting the name-check simply because he's occupying the seat furthest away from the stage. Quite rightly, Guy thinks he deserves our sympathy, so encourages 7,499 punters to give their fellow crowd member a huge round of applause. This whole routine might drift dangerously close to cheesy panto, but it does suggest that the band care about the welfare of their acolytes. It's a piece of theatre that Bono never considered employing in the NEC all those years back.

I wander down from my lofty perch to take in the view from the shop floor. The edge of the crowd is populated by a good number of couples seemingly too timid to get closer to the throng. Perhaps they've simply taken up this position in order to be first out of the door come home time. They look, just as I looked back at the NEC, distracted and distanced, too far away from the action to get completely caught up by the occasion. They seem to be hanging on for the big number, *One Day Like This*, chosen as the unofficial TV theme tune for William and Kate's wedding, despite it clearly detailing – from the very first line – a rare moment of clarity during a monumental hangover.

Here on the outskirts and on the fringes, even those wearing well-worn Elbow T-shirts from tours past, fans who've obviously been following them for a number of years, appear to be rather aloof from the proceedings. As I found at that Smiths Indeed gig, the talk in the men's toilets acts as a useful barometer of how well a gig is going. I pop to the loo and eavesdrop on a couple of punters who've obviously seen their heroes a good few times. Maybe they're just annoyed at *their* band now being loved by the nation; maybe they simply don't want to share them with these new admirers.

Fan #1 (left-hand urinal): What do you think? [What he really means is "Are you feeling as grumpy as I'm feeling?"]

Fan #2: (middle urinal): There's a lot of people here. ["I can't see the stage properly."]

Fan #1: They're doing a lot of the newer songs. ["Why won't they play the songs we want them to play, the ones that show we've supported them through thick and thin?"]

Fan #2: He's not as funny as he used to be. ["Where's all the direct banter with members of the crowd gone?"]

Me (right-hand urinal): Do you just not like the setting? ["Do you hold the popular view that an arena is, aside from a rain-lashed muddy festival field, the worst place to see a band?"]

Fan #1 and Fan #2 (together): Yes. ["Yes."]

I knew it. But, if you were Elbow, what could you do? Even if they shared my animosity for arena shows, their success has backed them into a corner. They're simply responding to demand. After all, it's not as if they're doing the bare minimum, taking the money and running. They're offering fans plenty of respect and courtesy. In no way could they be put in the same bracket as Guns N' Roses, whose notoriously abysmal time-keeping once saw them start their show at the MEN Arena at 11.15pm, quarter of an hour after the official curfew.

Although not denying themselves their hard-won moment in the sun, Elbow have shown themselves to have better manners than Axl Rose. After the show – and after those fans on the edge of the crowd have been served what they came for, in the form of the inevitable closer *One Day Like This* – Guy is very quickly out of his three-piece suit and back into his civvies. In checked shirt and jeans, he's sharing wisecracks and roll-ups at the stage door with the crew. And he's keen to express his take on the arena experience, how he adapts his performance to achieve the desired effect.

"If you're talking to 20,000 people, you don't dumb it down, but it has to be a simpler dialogue for everyone to get it. For the most part, it's one-way. It's me talking to them and asking for simple responses. At smaller gigs, you get into conversations with one character in the crowd. You maybe pick someone at the beginning. If we ever got a heckler, I'd end up talking to him in between every song. They just want to be part of the show." The concerns of Fan #2 in the gents' were indeed valid.

I mention that picking out Adrian Jones in the faraway seat was one way of shrinking the room, of making things cosier and more personal. "I have to talk to the crowd and how you communicate with them between the songs establishes what happens at that particular gig. It's the way that we know we've been to more than one place. It's the individual things that happen every night that make the show." He is well aware of the anonymity of the venues they're now cast to play – and how they could have a detrimental effect on how they themselves enjoy the shows.

"We were really oversubscribed for our first gig at the MEN Arena. We talked about putting the perpendicular, 180-degree seats on sale, the ones with restricted views. So, to make sure the people sat there didn't feel cheated, we turned them into the Elbow Choir. They each got their own Elbow Choir tunic and were an integral part of the show. You have to make sure they know that they're valued."

A pleasant chat with Elbow's erudite singer is one thing, but I've got other business to attend to. I head back into the auditorium and up the stairs again to retake a seat in the balcony. Everyone else has headed home and I have the place to myself. I sink into a grandstand seat for the second show of the night – the load-out.

If this afternoon was unhurried, the pace has been cranked up now. The house lights are up, exposing a choreographed flurry of activity. The stage barrier's already been removed and the catwalk is half the length it was ten minutes ago. The entire floor space has already been swept clean of thousands of discarded paper pint pots and plastic bottles, making the way clear for a fleet of forklifts and cherry pickers to be driven around the hall at frankly alarming speeds. I fully expect these fork-lifts to be transporting those hundreds and hundreds of flight cases from inside to out, where the fleet of artics are waiting to be loaded up. But then I witness something quite astounding.

The lights of an artic appear at the double doors leading out to the loading bay. They keep getting brighter and brighter. Surely not. Surely not. But yes. The truck is edging *through* the doors. Now its entire length is inside the hall. And now it's being driven across the dancefloor where it parks near the far wall. Not only have I never seen anything like that in a music venue before, but I also had absolutely no inkling that this was the nature of an arena load-out.

It doesn't stop there. A second artic squeezes through the doors and parks up next to the first. Then a third, then a fourth. The diesel fumes rise up to the balcony, but I'm too gripped by the spectacle to move elsewhere. Everyone is going in different directions – driving or lifting, pulling or pushing. The scene reminds me of many things. In its fast-changing tableau, it's a film put together using time-lapse photography. It also resem-bles a domino-toppling world record, the long, patient build-up undone by this sudden and rapid flattening. And it also reminds me of the multi-directional chaos of an Indian road junction. But no-one collides with either man or machinery. Tonight, once more, there are zero accidents on the job.

Everyone is in the groove. It's a vast jigsaw, one in which all 70 roadies know exactly where their pieces go and in what order. And each one is well aware that this is the time for action. They all seem extraordinarily ener-gised at this late hour, especially considering their dawn start. They must have each squeezed in a cat-nap or two at some point today, ten minutes' shut-eye leaned up against a flight case buying them an extra hour of energy come midnight.

After an hour of this weird, curiously addictive voyeurism – during which time more than one roadie has gazed upwards in my direction wondering why this nutter is sat in the balcony watching a few dozen blokes do some heavy lifting – I head off to the multi-storey car park. The queues at the ticket machine should just about be gone now. There's not much more to see anyhow. The arena has been stripped bare, relieved of her party clothes and make-up, of what made her pretty tonight. Like the band, the venue has tomorrow night off. Then Kylie's here on Friday.

I've never had a *Boy's Own*-style fascination for engin-eering or machines, but the orchestrated manoeuvres of Elbow's roadies and vehicles have sent my head spinning. In fact, they've sent my head spinning to such a degree that, as I drive through Cardiff's dark streets, I completely miss the turn for the motorway. And I don't realise the error of my ways until I'm halfway to Pontypridd, in *precisely* the opposite direction to Somerset. Neither Dave nor Johnny, with their in-built sat nav, would ever have made such a schoolboy error.

I turn the car around and, when I finally reach the motorway, soon catch up with a couple of Elbow's artics and one of the crew buses (sorry, Dave, "luxury coaches"). They're off on more high adventures in rock'n'roll. I'm a little envious of them, half-tempted to also leave the M4 at junction 24 and accompany them northbound. If for nothing else, I could certainly get used to that level of catering.

But then I remember the sheer physical graft, the 5.30am load-ins, the 1am load-outs, the snatched cat-naps, the months away from your own bed, from your family. I stay in my lane on the motorway. I've got my own tour of duty in the morning, after all. From home to school, school to nursery, nursery to home, and upstairs for my own 15-hour shift in front of a computer screen. That'll do for now.

While its logistics are fascinating, the arena show can never satisfy all those inside the room. A gig should be a spiritual – possibly intimate – experience that touches your soul and transports you elsewhere. Instead, it's become super-sized for mass consumption. Tonight, my heart did not race, my juices did not flow. Had I been closer to Guy Garvey's catwalk, maybe they would have, but I remain an outsider, a stranger in a strange land. My mojo is still missing.

What I need now is a place where the crowds are way, way smaller, where smooth-cornering tour buses don't venture, where there's no mini-industry set up around a single band. There may be spit. There may be sawdust. There's definitely a lot more soul.

9

GET YOUR KICKS ON THE A66

Destination: Live Lounge, Durham
Occasion: Half Man Half Biscuit gig
Miles travelled so far: 4,083
Follicly challenged musicians on stage: 3
Follicly challenged punters in audience: at least 60
Snow blizzards caught in while waiting for National Express
   coach home: 1

Jigsaws come in all sizes. If the logistical conundrum facing Elbow's crew every day is the equivalent of the 5,000-piece puzzle, the one playing out in front of me – on this snow-dusted, midnight Durham street – is more a toddler's shape-sorter. But it's one that's nonetheless baffling four middle-aged men: how to get a drum kit, two guitars, a bass, amps, the singer's wife and themselves into a hired Transit van while maintaining a level of comfort for the three-hour drive home.

This is more like it. If a fleet of articulated trucks makes the gigging experience too slick, too planned, too clinical, I've far more connection to this rougher, readier scenario. It's what I know. Even though I've never set foot within Durham's city limits before, I feel I'm on home ground.

The gear and personnel will fit in somehow. It always does. But there's none of the well-oiled choreography of an arena show load-out on display tonight; more a shove here and a nudge there, just enough so that the van's rear doors will shut. You couldn't even fit Elbow's mirrorball in the back of this Transit.

What's before me is a tableau that's been played out hundreds of thousands of times outside tens of thousands of venues. It's not remarkable. And it's probably why the scores of well-spoken Home Counties students, currently piling themselves into a late-closing bar next door, are oblivious to the scene. As the plentiful, 50-pence-piece-sized snowflakes float on the air, Sophie and Tim and Hugo and Hermione appear to be otherwise concerned with upholding the folk traditions of their adopted North-East – that is, seeing how few items of clothing can be worn in sub-zero conditions before the body's internal workings shut down.

It matters not that these students have got other things on their minds. Those four middle-aged men – collectively known as Merseyside's (and, for that matter, the world's) top musical satirists Half Man Half Biscuit – don't need a helping hand. They'll work out the puzzle themselves. After all, they fitted everything and everyone into the van for the journey up here from the Wirral.

Well, nearly everyone. Sadly, there was no room to squeeze in a well-upholstered music journalist from

Somerset for the trip up. So I made the north-by-north-east journey on the train instead, having elected to give the Honda – last heard making unholy grinding noises from three different locations on its undercarriage – a couple of days' rest and recuperation back home.

I took the Trans-Pennine Express, a train service whose prosaic stations – Stalybridge, Dewsbury, Northallerton – have yet to inspire Kraftwerk to pen a sequel to *Trans Europa Express*, their 1977 musical homage to cross-continental train travel. Curious that.

Despite the absence of a stirring soundtrack from Herrs Hütter and Schneider, it was by no means an unpleasant journey. Neither was it uneventful. For starters, there was the excitement of charging through the deep, dark tunnels underneath the Pennines, which I imagine feels not dissimilar to a journey into the centre of the Earth. At least, as long as that journey was organised by a regional train company seemingly unable to control the heating on their rolling stock.

Then there was that 15-minute delay at Leeds Station where the doors remained locked until British Transport Police's local constabulary arrived to deal with what the train conductor rather sweetly described as a bunch of "naughty boys" – known to the rest of us having our journey delayed as ASBO-deserving bell-ends – who were causing misery to passengers in another carriage.

By the time we joined the East Coast Main Line just south of York, the same train conductor had begun to spin tales of great woe over the PA, explaining how, with each mile we travelled northwards, the further we were venturing into some of the bleakest, snowiest weather known to humankind. If we believed her words, each of us was clutching a one-way ticket into a bottom-less chasm of no-return. She may well have been right. Through the greasy train windows, the closer to the North Pole we inched, the deeper, the crisper and the more even the snowfall.

This could have got serious. The woman with the refreshments trolley, hawking overpriced Kit-Kats and dispensing hot chocolate of a temperature that could remove your mouth's lining in a nanosecond, had wheeled away her mobile shop at an unidentified station some time before. That was our supplies gone. Should the train have hit a snowdrift in the wolf-infested badlands of the Thirsk area, we'd have had to rely on our instincts and wits for survival. And I only had an emergency packet of Werther's Originals to see me through the night.

When the train finally slid safely into Durham, the scene on the station platform partly appeased me, a delightful, snow-crusted picture postcard from more genteel times. But now the walk to the city centre is having the opposite effect – a sludgy, icy slide down the hill, starring a man in grip-free shoes with little physical coordination at the best of times. I'm very glad that the venue is just a few hundred yards away and, more importantly, on this side of the river. It means I won't risk plunging into the near-freezing depths of the Wear by having to negotiate the ice-rink pavements of the city's famous – and magnifi-cently named – Framwellgate Bridge.

Still, it takes more than a little snowfall and slushy streets to stop rock'n'roll. Isn't that what Twisted Sister once sang? If so, they were bang on the money. When I reach the venue, there's no sign of a half-expected 'Cancelled' poster. Instead, a van, with the contact details of a Liverpool hire company emblazoned on the side, is parked up outside. A good sign. The band are here, having conquered the well-gritted motorway network in record time.

Inside, I'm not overwhelmed by legions of crew. It's a lean venture – no tour manager, no sound man, no roadie. While their records are still spun to a healthy degree on the 6Music airwaves, Half Man Half Biscuit are still very much just doing it themselves. It's an endeavour that doesn't provide them all with a living wage. Neil the bass player works at the local museum, while Carl the drummer is surely the most rock'n'roll microbiologist around.

The only non-band members, aside from Nigel the singer's wife, are Geoff and his son Jesse. Geoff is the boss of Probe Plus, the one-man record label that's released the band's albums since the mid-'80s. His Toyota Corolla is parked outside, having chugged its way along the M62 stuffed to the gills with the 'merch' – mainly CDs and T-shirts, but also a few novelty items, such as Half Man Half Biscuit cigarette lighters. The pair have brought plenty of stock, quite possibly enough for every citizen of Durham to be wearing a HMHB T-shirt tomorrow morning. Jesse disappears behind a Hadrian's Wall of cardboard boxes that need unpacking before doors open.

Up on stage, the band are going through the ceremony of the soundcheck, a ritual they've undertaken hundreds of times. As ever, there are lengthy and protracted negotiations about the mix that the venue's soundman is giving them. Geoff breaks off from arranging the CD display to offer his opinions, with which I silently agree. For a band whose appeal lies almost exclusively in its sure-footed wordplay, the mix, even to my untrained ears, sounds distinctly muddy. If I didn't already know precisely 94% of their back catalogue – making me well up to scratch with their finer lyrical subtleties – I wouldn't be able to tell what the hell Nigel was on about come showtime. You just can't hear the words.

With only those Werther's Originals on me (which I'm being very disciplined about, as if the packet bears the warning Only Open in the Event of an Emergency), I'm a little peckish. I've not eaten anything meaningful since a limp and disappointing houmous sandwich at Manchester Piccadilly and I find a similarly flaccid offering in a shop a few doors down from the venue. Unlike at the Motorpoint Arena, there'll be no restaurant-quality, three-course feed for me tonight. There's no team of chefs, no excessive backstage rider. In fact, it appears there's no rider at all, if a single empty Pringles tube in the dressing room is anything to go by. Instead, the band shuffle off to the pub over the road to find their own dinner.

It's a poor promoter who doesn't at least make even the mildest attempt at keeping a band fed and watered. An act that's had a little bit of TLC will invariably be a happier act. (A bit of love and care, I mean, not the musical charms of the celebrated vocal trio from Atlanta.) And a happy act will put in a much better performance than an act grown grumpy through a lack of sustenance, stomachs rumbling, throats dry.

The band are probably halfway through a microwaved lasagne in the pub when the doors of the venue open for business. There's no priority queue for those signed up to a particular mobile phone provider. No ridiculously early finish so the promoter can squeeze in a club night afterwards and double his money. No nonsense at all. Cash on the door, stamp on the hand, beer at an affordable price. Exactly as it should be.

The crowd filing in is as I expect. The band's songs speak on behalf of a precise constituency – men in their forties and fifties for whom the modern world is not only illogical and unravelling, but also presided over by a confederacy of dunces. The songs speak to people like me. But worry not: these musical diatribes don't veer remotely close to Clarkson/Grumpy Old Men territory, the domain of sour-faced gentlemen of a certain age getting disproportionately apoplectic about gobsmackingly trivial affairs.

Half Man Half Biscuit's despatches are subtler, wiser, more considered. And undoubtedly funnier. These songs reproach us for being distracted by trivia ("While you're capturing the zeitgeist/They're widening the motorway"). They despair about the effects of ever-thinning popular culture (*He Who Would Valium Take*). And, most crucially, they warn about the everyday challenge of taking a primate with behavioural difficulties to an interior design exhibition (the fabulous *Took Problem Chimp To Ideal Home Show*).

As they rip through the idiocy of our times, Nigel's razor-sharp barbs are matched by his nimble wordplay. Lyrics tell of "drive-by shoutings", while reports come in that "Nero fiddles while Gordon Burns". (At this juncture, I feel compelled to offer my own similarly constructed witticism should the band ever be in need of a lyric about ex-*Playschool* presenters: Jeremy Irons but Brian Cant. Boom boom.)

And the titles Nigel comes up with, both for album and song, can't be bettered – *Trouble Over Bridgwater, CSI Ambleside, Twenty-Four-Hour Garage People, The*

Light At The End Of The Tunnel (Is The Light Of An Oncoming Train…). If I were a believer in the Honours List – and, indeed, had some say in the matter – I'd mark him down for a knighthood simply for coming up with the line "There's a man with a mullet going mad with a mallet in Millets".

In a parallel world, Nigel would be employed by Radio 4's live arts programme *Loose Ends* to close out proceedings every week with a witty and topical song. The rest of the working week would then be spent alongside Susie Dent in *Countdown*'s Dictionary Corner, coolly trading witticisms with Richard Whiteley's latest successor. Like a latter-day Gyles Brandreth, but without the smugness, the jumpers and the despicable Toryism.

I imagine Nigel would hate any approach from *Loose Ends* – although I suspect he might be a bit warmer if the people from *Countdown* came knocking on his door. Imaginary media offers aside, what I'm trying to say is that, in a right-thinking world, this is a man who should be lauded as a national treasure. Yes, I'm well aware that 'national treasure' is an excessively (and therefore ever less meaningfully) employed phrase, the overuse of which I've just added to. It's just that this Birkenhead boy is far more deserving of a nation's adoration than Nigella Lawson or Gok Wan or James effing May from *Top Gear*.

But Nigel Blackwell is the enemy of ambition. Playing a standalone gig every six weeks or so, he's not one to bathe himself in the dazzling glare of limelight. Nor to pursue the shameless cash-in with wildly greedy eyes. I dare say that there would be plenty of promoters willing to pay top dollar for Nigel and the band to play their 1985 breakthrough album *Back In The DHSS* live in its entirety, to dust off that record's totemic songs – anthems like *Fucking 'Ell It's Fred Titmus* and *99% Of Gargoyles Look Like Bob Todd* that have, strangely, yet to be covered by the warbling wannabes on *The X Factor*.

Back in the dressing room while the support band is on, Nigel reveals to me – and to the rest of the band, actually – that he did recently receive an offer to do one of their old records in its entirety. In 2002, the band put out an album called *Cammell Laird Social Club*, a record that, while alluding to the title of the multi-million-selling, Ry Cooder-enhanced *Buena Vista Social Club* album, transplanted the action from steamy Havana to the misty Wirral, specifically to the social club of the peninsula's most famous shipbuilding firm.

Three members of the actual social club, inspired by the vogue of bands playing whole albums live, had been in touch to ask if Nigel and the band would be interested in doing exactly the same with that particular album. He politely declined, his first reason being an artistic one. "We don't really write albums as albums," he explains. "Our albums are just the latest batch of 12 songs we've got at that time." The second reason was more practical. "I don't know if we even *could* do *Cammell Laird Social Club*. Sitting here now, I couldn't tell you what the first track was!

"Plus, I've never had the inclination to go backwards. And there's that rebellious streak – 'We don't want to do that because everyone else is doing it'. That's why I never smoked pot. Because everybody else was doing it." This is a band that's unashamedly free range in an industry that prefers intense battery farming.

Tomorrow night, Primal Scream – contemporaries of Half Man Half Biscuit from the *NME*'s *C86* compilation cassette of 25 years previous – will be filling London's Olympia by retreading their classic album *Screamadelica*. Olympia can accommodate a good few thousand people. Durham's Live Lounge holds a bit less. But Nigel seems unconcerned about the stature of the venues they play.

On the other side of the thin dressing room wall, the support band rumble into action, intent on playing at an interview-unfriendly loud level. Nigel leans in to make sure the dictaphone picks him up as he explains why the band only do these one-off gigs, electing to reject any offers of proper multi-date tours. Even gigs on successive nights are hens'-teeth rare. "I love being at home," he reveals modestly. "I've got a dog and a very happy home life. I don't want to go away from that too much. None of the neighbours have got a clue that I'm in a band. And that suits me.

"But I think the main reason is that, if we went on a 21-date tour, by gig 14 I'm sure I'd be on automatic pilot. And I wouldn't want to do that. To go on three weeks in a row, it would be that 'If it's Tuesday, it's Belgium' kind of thing. We could do more gigs, but it would take the fun out of it. Like tonight – we've had a nice drive up, but if we were doing that all the time, it would annoy us night after night after night."

Not even the lure of cashing in while live music is booming, and while the nostalgia train is still in the station, can change his working practices. "I was so long on the dole that I learned to live without money. Or with just enough. After we've done a gig, I just have a bit more. It keeps me alright and it pays the mortgage. I'm happy. I can get up each day and decide what I want to do with that day. That suits me."

Half an hour or so later, Nigel steers the band on stage to a full-voiced welcome, as if he were leading his beloved Tranmere Rovers out at Wembley for the Johnstone's Paint Trophy final. Interspersed with the kind of one-to-one banter that Guy Garvey lamented was now missing from Elbow's performances, HMHB classic follows HMHB classic – *Bad Losers On Yahoo Chess*, *Running Order Squabble Fest*, *All I Want For Christmas Is A Dukla Prague Away Kit*...

The loyalists are thoroughly on-side. So am I. In the age of video screens the size of houses and light shows that give the aurora borealis a run for its money, it's confirmation that four ordinary-looking blokes with guitars and drums can still take you somewhere else, to a place where nothing else matters. Mortgages, office politics, underperforming pension funds. All of life's strains and woes are unloaded, jettisoned, forgotten. For the next 90 minutes or so, at least.

During the much-loved *Joy Division Oven Gloves*, I feel a thwack around the back of my head. I spin round but it's quickly obvious there's not going to be any trouble. The offender raises a hand in my direction by way of an apology. But the hand is hidden inside a pair of oven gloves that he's customised to add the cover artwork of *Unknown Pleasures*, Joy Division's debut album. Yes, that's right, he's fashioned his own Joy Division oven gloves, just to wave maniacally for the three minutes and 13 seconds it takes for the band to whip through this particular crowd favourite. He's not alone in his tribute. His mate next to him has made his own pair too.

Such antics are proof of the partisanship of this crowd, one that doesn't miss a syllable as they sing along en masse to every tune. At HMHB gigs, they wear their hearts on their sleeves. And their oven gloves on their hands. But this loyalty isn't only articulated through the redesign of kitchen-based protective wear, as a glimpse at the internet will reveal. One fansite consists of full transcriptions and in-depth analysis of every Blackwell lyric ever recorded. The site goes by the attractive strapline of "179 pop songs picked over by pedants". My kind of people.

Tonight's audience are my kind of people too. They're not distracted from the task at hand, unlike those fidgety, half-engaged types on the edge of Elbow's audience. These are not floating voters who've come here to chat about their recent city break in Tallinn or next weekend's barbecue plans, while some band fills in the pauses in their conversations. Attention is full, commitment unswerving. Just as with those head-banging long-hairs at Bloodstock.

Commitment is also unswerving when it comes to that – admittedly less than arduous – gigging schedule. The hardcore portion of this crowd travel to all the shows, hitting the highway every six weeks or so to meet up with their fellow fanatics, whether the destination is Bath or Bilston, Cambridge or Kendal. I purr my approval. I could do with a hobby and there are far more unappealing pastimes than joining the merry HMHB caravan around the country. Like pigeon racing, or cross-stitch. I like a road trip too, at least when the Honda can be relied upon not to give up the ghost a couple of hundred miles from home.

Such expeditions would be even better if I could muster a few of my pals to come along for the ride. It would certainly show an allegiance to a band that I hadn't declared since the late '90s when Jane and I – pre-kids – would hopelessly trail Gorky's Zygotic Mynci around the lower half of the country, from Tenby's De Valence Pavilion to the Royal Festival Hall and all points in between. My attraction to them centred on their slow, mournful ballads. I suspect Jane's interest was more to do with Euros Childs, their boyishly handsome, lavishly coiffured singer.

My keenness to join the HMHB ultras is cemented when – at the T-shirt stall afterwards, following a high-value, 28-song set – I fall into conversation with one of these hardcore acolytes. John's up from South Yorkshire. It's the sixth time he's seen the band in the last 12 months – not bad seeing as how it's only their eighth gig of the year. And, also, seeing as how he's the father of an eight-month-old baby daughter. I suppose the fact that your favourite band only does a gig every six weeks or so helps when it comes to negotiating a night off from the nappies.

"I don't follow football," he reasons, "but mates of mine who do are neglecting their domestic duties pretty much every weekend during the season. That's the justification I give my wife, anyhow. She can't see the appeal of the band – she's more of a Coldplay lass – so she doesn't understand why I'm off on these jaunts every few weeks, especially in this weather. Often I'm doing them alone if I can't persuade someone to join me. They can be round-trips of a couple of hundred miles, but it's a price I'm happy enough to pay. No-one I work with can understand this devotion, but in places like this, I can be among like-minded souls. We're all singing our hearts out." John pauses. "This band are our team."

He's sold it to me. Tonight, and for other nights to come, I'm crossing over to his side of the street. This armchair HMHB fan just became a metaphorical season-ticket holder. I bid John farewell, declaring my intentions to meet up with him again at the band's next gig in Holmfirth. Comparatively, it'll be a home game for him, but another long schlep from Somerset for me. But it will also be my birthday, so perhaps I'll treat myself to another ride on the Trans-Pennine Express. Maybe even splash out on an inexpensive B&B. John slides out into the snowy night, a new HMHB T-shirt tucked under his arm.

He's not the only one updating his wardrobe tonight. Geoff's stall is doing pretty tidy business. While loyalists rifle through the crates of vinyl, eager to plug holes in their record collections, others are renewing their favourite T-shirts as life forces them to shift a size upwards. M to L, L to XL, XL to XXL.

But however tidy the business that the stall is doing, however much lighter the boxes are when they're loaded back into Geoff's car, there's still not enough room in the Corolla for an extra passenger. With all the instruments and merchandise squeezed in, the two-vehicle, Merseyside-bound entourage again leaves without me, the soothing songs of the aforementioned Gorky's Zygotic Mynci on the van stereo. I'm forced to use the only method of getting out of Durham once the trains have stopped running – the overnight National Express coach to London. The red-eye.

The 'red-eye' is a phrase usually associated with a time-zone-warping flight to Tokyo. My journey is decidedly less exotic. Right at this moment, Elbow are probably cruising along some autobahn in enviable luxury, their only concerns being which games console to play with next or which brand of expensive bottled beer to crack open. Here on my bus, there are no luxury facilities, no plentiful refreshment. Instead, sitting opposite, there's a bear of a man of, I'm guessing, Scandinavian extraction, snoring for queen and country. His blond, droopy moustache is vibrating with each porcine inhalation. This is going to be fun. Six long hours of bug-eyed, insomniac frustration await, not aided by the mild tinnitus I've developed from standing right in front of the speaker stack. No sleep 'til Milton Keynes Coachway, as the Beastie Boys almost certainly didn't have it.

I'm awake for the first half-hour at least, but then – somewhere along the A66, between Darlington town centre and the next motorway junction – I drop off and don't wake up until dawn, just as the bus is gliding past Lord's cricket ground in north-west London. My Danish friend is still fast asleep. But no matter how numb my bum is and how long-winded the journey's been (and it'll be another four hours or so until I reach my doorstep), investing so much time and effort for two hours of live music hasn't felt unnatural. There's a familiar tang about it. Racing through my brain, pulsing through my vein. It's the returning taste of gig addiction.

It's been so long since I was such a dirty stop-out, since I was led so astray by rock'n'roll. Back then, it was par for the course. Missing the last train home. Scrounging lifts off strangers or stowing away on the 4am mail train with no idea of where it's actually heading. Getting back home just as everyone's off to work or college. It's this spontaneous, fly-by-the-seat-of-the-pants approach – of both band and gig-goer – that I want to experience some more.

I could get used to it. Clearly, I've just been looking in the wrong places thus far – in enormodomes, in forests, in the grounds of stately homes. Turns out it was where it always was.

I now need to feed this returning addiction by travelling back to another familiar place. I'm heading east, to the musically rich home county of Billy Bragg, of Blur, of Dr Feelgood, of The Prodigy. Specifically, to the place where I was first conscripted as a foot soldier in the service of rock'n'roll. Where I served my live music apprenticeship. And where I became a dab hand at solving those Ford Transit-based jigsaw puzzles.

10

THIS USED TO BE MY PLAYGROUND

Destination: Essex University Students' Union, Colchester
Occasion: Eliza Doolittle show during freshers' week
Miles travelled so far: 4,526
Miles travelled along memory lane: innumerable
Embarrassing, attention-grabbing pratfalls: 1
Post-gig 'rat-burgers' consumed: 0

Alan McGee is knocking on the door. Alan McGee is coming into my office. Alan McGee is asking me a favour.

Tonight's support band trail in his wake. They are called Lush and will, in a few years' time, enjoy a little chart success. But tonight they're being paid just 50 quid to warm up this evening's crowd for headliners The House Of Love. So Alan McGee is asking me for a few beers to ease the blow of them playing for such a modest purse. I run a hand through my quiff. Fair dos, I reckon. A few cans of unchilled, piss-weak lager are the least I can find for them. I might even throw in some homemade cheese-and-pickle sandwiches too.

Even if this request for a little light refreshment were remotely unreasonable, I'm not exactly in a position to argue the toss. After all, Alan McGee – tall, Glaswegian and more than a wee bit intimidating – is something of a player. In a few years' time, discovering and signing Oasis to his Creation Records label will make his bank manager a very happy man. Even tonight – nearly a decade before Tony Blair very publicly hosts him and those gobby Gallagher brothers in the hallowed halls of Number 10 – McGee is, aside from John Peel and whoever's currently editing the *NME*, the most influential person in indie music. And here he is, asking little old me a favour.

It is 2 June 1989, I am 20 years old and the sign on the office door tells anyone passing that I am, apparently, the Entertainments Officer for Essex University Students' Union. The sign is particularly shiny. I was elected just last month. And, whisper it quietly, I am woefully, *woefully* underqualified for such a job.

Let's look at the evidence. As I've already admitted, before I arrived at university just eight months previously, I'd only been to four gigs. Until then, and indeed for some time after, the vocabulary of live music – a world of 'load-ins', 'drum risers', 'PA stacks' – was an alien tongue. I was an outsider, a stranger in a strange land.

Secondly, had I been remotely inclined or brave enough to play hardball with an agent, a tour manager or scary old Alan McGee, my previous work experience would have stood me in the worst possible stead. Up until then, my employment history ran to a few years' service as a paperboy, the odd summer spent stacking supermarket shelves and – worst of all – picking tomatoes in the sauna-like temperatures of a giant greenhouse. My negotiation skills extended no further than asking my supervisor whether I could take an early lunch.

The situation was, quite frankly, ridiculous. What other industry would put a wet-behind-the-ears novice in a role of relative power, responsible for five-figure budgets and at the mercy of merciless, bloodsucking booking agents?

They must have been mad.

❧ ❧ ❧ ❧ ❧

More than two decades later, it's a warm, welcoming October evening when I pull into the visitors' car park. All is peaceful here on the outskirts of Colchester, the only sounds coming from a mildly committed football match on the Astroturf and from a moped's buzzing engine, carrying its rider home after a day of Descartes and Derrida.

I saunter down the hill towards the main university buildings, past empty tennis courts onto which the first autumn leaves are falling. To my left are a couple of Eastern Bloc-style tower blocks. I can still remember what they're called. One stands in tribute to – and takes the name of – libertarian philosopher/serial philanderer Bertrand Russell. The other is called Eddington, disappointingly named in honour of eminent astrophysicist Arthur rather than comedy actor Paul.

I'm quietly impressed with my powers of recall. Many years have passed since I last clapped eyes on these tower blocks, but little has changed. The procession of sallow-

faced students heading back towards their accommodation, invariably to rustle up some less-than-delicious
instant noodles, is the same as it ever was, their stilted
conversations confirming that they only met their flatmates a day or two before. And, with these stilted conversations largely limited to what A-level results they got this
past summer, the scene is unmistakable. This is freshers'
week at a provincial British university.

One thing is different. On my first day here in the
late '80s, as I sped towards the students' union offices to
sign up for the Ents crew, I slowed only to appreciate the
artistic mosaics of posters that were everywhere – freshly
minted calls to action for the recognition of Palestine,
the repeal of Section 28, the release of Nelson Mandela.
Mostly I was ogling the gig posters, seeing which bands
had been enticed up to this faraway corner of England's
most maligned county, which bands would provide the
soundtrack to my first term.

That's what's missing around here now. Posters. Posters
commanding you to attend this meeting. Posters recruiting
you for that rally. Posters announcing next Saturday's live
music turn. I stick my head around the door of the Union
Bar. Once upon a time, its walls were crammed, from
skirting board to ceiling, with artwork of varying degrees
of professionalism. A glance around the room provided a
barometer reading of campus life, of the level and degree
of student activity.

Now these walls stand naked, wearing only a recent
paint job in one of those neutral, supposedly inoffensive
beige shades with artificially rustic names – Oatmeal
Sunset or Autumn Horsehair. The barometer needle has
nothing to show. Where's the commitment? Where's the

activism? It's not as if there aren't any causes left to fight for. Why, the Lib Dems' unforgivable U-turn over tuition fees has made sure of that. But there is a reason for the paucity of gig posters. Tonight's show – by pop starlet-in-waiting Eliza Doolittle – is the only, *only* proper gig from a proper live band here at Essex this whole term. From the first week in October to the middle of December. Just the one.

It's not as if this has always been the way. Although not on the itinerary of every single feted touring act, Essex University traditionally punched above its weight when it came to gigs. In the late '70s, the BBC filmed the likes of AC/DC and Lindisfarne playing here for its series *Rock Goes to College*. BBC Four still seems particularly keen on the Lindisfarne show, dusting off the recording from time to time to show to insomniac – and possibly herbally refreshed – bearded types at a time of night when all the other channels have reverted to five-hour-long gambling shows.

A decade later, class acts such as The Smiths and REM stopped off here – I've got the bootleg tapes to prove it. And the night after I first came here on a campus open day, Robert Plant was due to play. On the US leg of the same tour, Plant played Madison Square Garden as well as two nights at the Red Rocks Amphitheatre in Colorado. But, just a couple of months before, he also performed in Essex's converted underground car park.

Those halcyon days appear to be consigned to the history books. It seems that B-class DJs, club nights and booze promotions are now all it takes to keep the campus entertained. When it comes to steam-powered instruments being played by steam-powered musicians, tonight's show from Eliza and her band is all that Essex's students are going to get this side of Christmas.

I hate myself for adopting a never-in-my-day stance, but I simply have to compare and contrast this sorry state of affairs with that array of gig posters I encountered in my own freshers' week. Lined up and ready to play for my delectation in the autumn term of 1988 were:

- Derek B / Pop Will Eat Itself
- Westworld
- Cookie Crew
- The Men They Couldn't Hang / A House
- Steel Pulse
- The Proclaimers
- Roy Harper
- Roachford
- Wee Papa Girl Rappers
- The Bootleg Beatles

Those are just the ones I remember.

Now, anyone reading this who at the time was studying in London, Manchester, Leeds, Liverpool, Birmingham, Newcastle or even little old Norwich may well chortle at the quantity and quality of this line-up. In these cities, *NME* cover stars seemed to play on a near-nightly basis. But, for a very small provincial university on the fringes of a comparatively small provincial town, this list wasn't at all bad. And it certainly outshone a single Eliza Doolittle gig to the nth degree.

I head upstairs to the students' union offices. The corridor looks very familiar – the same linoleum flooring, the same strip lighting that was always under threat whenever we played a little game of indoor frisbee at an ungodly post-gig hour. This anonymous corridor holds extra significance for me – it's where I first met Jane, a blonde vision in short skirt, black tights and 14-hole Dr Martens boots, and accessorised by badges declaring twin appreciations for Vladimir Lenin and the anti-vivisection movement. If Jane had done a little better in her A-levels, and I'd done a bit worse, neither of us would have been packing our bags for Colchester – meaning, of course, that our two sons and heirs wouldn't exist. I'd applied to Essex because it set a comparatively low academic bar for its applicants and because it boasted a campus radio station upon whose listenership I could force my record collection. No radio station would have meant no application, no Jane, no Finn, no Ned. That was my *Sliding Doors* moment.

The far end of the union corridor always felt like home. The last door on the right – the one that Alan McGee once firmly rapped on – led into the Ents office, just past the staff room where I once spent two full hours trying to microwave De La Soul's Chinese meals to anything beyond room temperature. (I failed. Their response? "We're not eating that shit. Where's the nearest McDonalds?")

I wish I'd kept the nameplate from the door – NIGEL TASSELL, ENTERTAINMENTS OFFICER. Not bad for a 20-year-old ex-paperboy. I bet someone at ICI or General Electric has to put in a couple of decades of devoted, brown-nosing service before they get remotely close to that honour. All I had to do was gain the approval of those few hundred students who could be bothered to get out of bed and vote in the campus elections before the polls closed at 6pm.

Most slept on, but I got enough votes to carry a majority. It was a victory not won by dazzling oratory at the hustings, nor by making wildly optimistic promises of booking The Rolling Stones for the end-of-term all-nighter. No, my Obama-like sweep to power was chiefly the result of having a surname that lent itself to a vaguely memorable campaign slogan: No Hassle With Tassell.

Thus far, you might have been under the impression that I was courageously leading the whole shebang single-handedly, steering through the choppy waters of organising 3,000 students' social lives guided only by a precocious, hitherto untapped instinct. In fact, I had the luxury of a safety net. Someone else's name was on the door as well. The students' union had made the prudent decision not to place all its financial eggs in the basket of someone just a few months out of his teens and wisely also employed a full-time, permanent and – most crucially – *experienced* entertainments manager. His name was Josh Smaller.

Josh was an Andrew Ridgeley lookalike of Indian parentage who'd gone to school with The Cure's Robert Smith. A veteran of gig promotion at Goldsmiths College, he was a complete rock – steely when facing down the brick shithouse bouncers we employed cash-in-hand, highly imaginative when it came to marketing and promotion.

Josh taught me plenty, not least the twin virtues of frugality and self-sufficiency. After all, why simply pick up the phone and take two minutes to book bulbous-headed comedy musician Frank Sidebottom to host your Battle of the Bands competition, when you can literally spend three weeks patiently fashioning your own papier-mâché head and honing your best Timperley accent so that you can impersonate him on the night and save some cash?

And although it was our names on the office door, this was no two-man show. While far from generous in size, the office was also the daytime hangout of choice for the entire Ents crew, a retreat from the rigour of intellectual pursuit and where an afternoon of music, banter and merriment was yours in exchange for a 20-minute shift with the paste bucket.

The room could comfortably accommodate eight or so of us at any one time, as long as one or two didn't mind perching on top of the safe that was cemented to the floor. Thinking back, this was a pretty large safe. Ambitiously large, in fact, considering the decidedly meagre takings we were adept at collecting. Cementing it to the floor certainly appears to have been an overly cautious measure. (The blood runs cold at this point when I remember we hosted An Evening With Ian Botham one Saturday night, hiring out, at great expense, the university's largest lecture theatre for the occasion. It turned out there were only 26 Ian Botham fans in the whole of Essex. A whole term was spent recouping that particular loss.)

I loved our Ents office. It was scruffy, it was scuzzy. And it certainly carried its own odour. The chairs wore the bullet-holes of fag burns, while the murky brown carpet handily disguised a multitude of sins. The place resembled a teenage lad's bedroom rather than a proper grown-ups' office. Unlike most teenage lads' bedrooms, though, there wasn't a single traffic cone to be seen. We'd gone one better. In the corner was a six-foot-high temporary bus stop complete with concrete base, a souvenir liberated from the streets of Chelmsford after a works outing to see The Sandkings play at the town's YMCA.

And spewing across the floor, like primordial ooze, was an ever-multiplying mass of demo tapes, cassettes sent to us by eager young pups who all had their eyes on one of those 50-quid support slots. Maybe the chance to open for West Yorkshire goths Ghost Dance or to suffer the slings and arrows (and possibly bottles of wee) of Dogs D'Amor's unwashed fanbase. Along with a cassette, hopes and dreams poured out of each jiffy bag. As ashamed as I am to admit, there was certainly far more importance attached to each package when it disappeared into the postbox than when it landed on our desk. We just received so many. And among their number would have been a demo from a local outfit called Seymour, just another band whose tape we paid scant attention to and whose career we never helped advance.

No matter. They would soon change their name to Blur.

The Ents crew were a gang. We were family. And we came in all shapes and sizes, from hefty Asian lads from Coventry to diminutive female students who called the Cayman Islands home. A cross-tribe gang of goths, indie kids, soul boys and the musically unaffiliated. And, for the tricky technical bits, electrical engineering students.

We were united by an eagerness to participate, to give our time up for free, to not just be passengers during our university years. The task that needed doing might be heading into town armed with paste bucket and posters. It might be demonstrating some hitherto untapped prowess with a blank piece of paper, a sheet of Letraset letters and a photocopier to 'design' some rudimentary flyers. More often than not, it meant being relied upon to stay sober until one in the morning just to push a trail of heavy flight cases into the back of a Luton van. The work was by no means glamorous. Indeed, arguably the most glamorous moment of my whole tenure was accompanying rubber-faced comedian Phil Cool for a pre-gig jacket potato. Actually, come to think of it, that particular high point may well have been trumped by accidentally catching a glimpse of Mark E Smith's nob while he was having a wee by the stage door.

The work, though, was worthwhile and rewarding. Unpaid time and unsocial hours, but driven along by a camaraderie I've never really experienced since in my working life, generated by this wonky brigade operating out of this wonky office.

But the Ents department doesn't live at the end of the corridor any more. I double-back on myself, retrace my steps and find the current office where the campus radio station used to be. To be fair, it was easy to miss. It's a very small room. In fact, it's an office that can barely accommodate more than a couple of people. There's no way even a quarter of our crew could have squeezed into here.

Its current resident, the incumbent Entertainments Manager, is Malcolm Laquis-Alden. When I see his name on the door, I immediately picture some ridiculously young, annoyingly confident public-school type, more equipped to hosting ultra-glamorous, Cristal-lubricated nightclub parties than down-and-dirty rock'n'roll shows.

My presumption turns out to be misplaced. Not only is Malcolm a family man the same age as me, he was also in the same class in the same Colchester school as Damon Albarn and Graham Coxon, the town's most celebrated musical alumni, the boys who once made up one half of Seymour. Bearing in mind Josh's own future hit-making school-mate, perhaps a sign should be put up above the door: You Don't Have to Have Gone to School with a Rock Star to Work Here... But It Helps.

Malcolm's also put in plenty of time touring on the road himself. So, as someone with such decent live music credentials, isn't he frustrated by only putting on a single gig this term? "I know we're sitting on a goldmine," he sighs, before detailing where the Essex live experience came off the rails.

In the late '80s and early '90s, the county of Essex was a seedbed for rave culture, fed and watered by scores of authority-baiting illegal gatherings just off the M25 and by the scene's totem figures The Prodigy, who hailed from the otherwise musically benign town of Braintree. The students' union at Essex aligned itself with this cultural wave, hiring the main hall out – with growing frequency – to external promoters. The punters poured in. So did the cash.

But despite these regular deposits into its coffers, the union was suffering. Young men with decks and samplers were favoured over young men with electric guitars, so the venue removed itself from the radar of bands and booking agents alike. Dance music had inflicted some serious damage on the campus's appetite for gigs. "We came off the live circuit then," Malcolm observes. "We fell off the map. Being offered bands became more and more sporadic."

The situation hasn't improved greatly since. "We still put on the big gigs now, but they're infrequent. We're at the stage where we can't put smaller, unknown bands on. Students now listen to the A-list on Radio 1. If anything's a bit leftfield or if they don't know the name of the artist, they won't turn up. They won't take a risk. You could put a band on who might be brilliant, but nobody knows them. And you have an empty venue."

While students' unions in bigger towns and cities can still take artistic gambles, Malcolm is a victim of geography, of population size and of student numbers. "We're only just hitting 10,000 students here. Nottingham has 35,000. They just open their doors. Their venues are full every single night without having to do much." Added to this, 40% of Essex's 10,000 are international students, many from South-east Asia, most of whom, Malcolm notes, "haven't a clue who our artists are".

Not only is the student pound spread somewhat thinner nowadays, what with the introduction of tuition fees in recent years, but student behaviour after dark has changed too. Essex's young academics are simply not in and around the students' union building at the time that bands would traditionally go on stage. "There's a massive Tesco Extra just down the road," Malcolm reports. "I've seen students pushing trolleys of cut-price alcohol back up the hill. They go to the halls of residence, get half-cut and then come down to the venues at ridiculous times – at 12 or one o'clock in the morning. That's the modern culture." They're venturing out at a time when most music venues have locked their doors for the night.

Malcolm's words are littered with marketing speak – "business plans", "leadership management", "going forward" – phrases I'd normally scarper from. And the most conspicuous item in the office isn't a half-inched bus stop sign; it's a collection of wipe-boards detailing Malcolm's latest marketing strategies. But I think I can forgive him for these. Competing with distractions that hadn't yet been invented at the time of my spell here – the internet, social media, budget-priced supermarket alcohol – means that successfully entertaining a university campus is now far from a simple endeavour.

Josh and I had little competition for our students' attentions; accordingly, our market research was pretty much non-existent. The whole operation was bare-boned – no computer was needed (nor, indeed, was available). All we had was a phone, a calculator and a desk, onto which phone messages and agents' offers were scribbled. We booked acts according to hunch and intuition, usually based on a 30-second conversation that would go something like this:

Josh: What do you reckon about [insert name of decidedly average late-'80s indie band here]?
Me: Did a good Peel session last week. How much?
Josh: £550. Bringing their own support.
Me: Not too bad. They'd definitely pull 300. Maybe even get 350 in. Fiver absolute tops on the door, though. £4 advance?

Cue frenzied tapping of calculator keys, using our (usually) fail-safe equation – however many tickets you sell in advance, you'll sell the same amount again on the door. A campus audience, particularly in a squaddie town, is very much a captive audience.

Josh: 150 at £4. That's 600 quid. 150 at £5. Another 750 quid.

A quick subtraction of our fixed costs (PA hire, publicity, security, sandwiches…) before arriving at our scientifically deduced profit margin.

Josh: Yup, that's fine. I'll call the agent back on Friday.

Malcolm's marketing strategies quite possibly produce fatter profits for the union. Indeed, tonight he's coordinating what economists would describe as four separate income streams – a gig, a club night and two shows from that staple of freshers' week, the comedy hypnotist. No wonder the team are communicating by walkie-talkie. There's a lot to coordinate. Malcolm's is a tightly run ship and this is an admirable workload. We'd never have been able to cope with such an itinerary.

One of his charges comes into the office, not to kick back and relax as our guys and girls used to, but to report on tonight's numbers, on the "footfall". Rather distressingly, she's wearing – as are, I'll later discover, the rest of the team – a colour-coordinated polo shirt. Hers has 'Team Leader' embroidered across the chest.

My initial reaction is one of horror. Even if we'd had the inclination to force our Ents crew into uniform, we'd have received a scalding volley of potty-mouthed abuse in return. Under no imaginable circumstances would we have been able to persuade these young men to swap leather jackets and band T-shirts for the attire of choice of the professional golfer.

Today's Ents crew appear to have no problem with being kitted out in coordinated polo shirts. For them, it's just a paid job and it's just a uniform. Yes, they're *paid*. Not volunteers doing it for love; they're earning extra cash to see them through college, to keep those student loan applications to a minimum. And, of course, to provide ballast on their post-graduation CVs.

When it comes to the more technical and more physical jobs, where it was once keen amateurs and enthusiastic volunteers, it's now specialist staff performing specialist duties. No more the eager fresher deployed to undertake tasks beyond their ken. In the age of extensive health and safety certification – and the ever more sophisticated hardware used in lighting and sound – training is imperative. "You can't just take Joe Bloggs student off the street with no experience," explains Malcolm. "You've got to be ticketed for everything, from changing a plug upwards. There's all this legislation and litigation that will come down on you if one of your guys has an accident, whether he gets electrocuted or falls off a ladder or whatever. Now, before you press a button, you've got to have a card that says you can press that button effectively well."

Health and safety was of scant concern in the late '80s. We just got on with it and muddled through. Not that I want to paint my time, unburdened by legislation and paperwork, as some kind of golden age in live music production. After all, I daresay that the chimneysweeping industry still curses the day when the soul went out of their trade, when it was reluctantly accepted that cheap pre-pubescent labour being sent up the nation's flues might not be the safest, nor morally watertight, way for their business to be run. A firmer grasp on professionalism is probably no bad thing. Health and safety legislation can be a force for good – a workforce with the same number of limbs at the end of the working day as at the start is a happy workforce. Not even knee-jerk rent-a-shit Richard Littlejohn can dispute that.

While the Union Bar has become blander and the Ents office smaller, the main hall is the one place I really care about. I'm not at all bothered that it's been renamed. Back then, its ludicrously unfashionable name – the Dancehall – conjured up images of maiden aunts and chinking crockery and afternoon tea dances. The reality was a venue choking on cigarette smoke and populated by fans of Senseless Things throwing themselves around in puddles of cheap lager and, most probably, piss.

It's now called Sub-Zero, an edgier name that also reflects its subterranean location, that former underground car park buried deep in the bowels of a campus university. Its new name is a definite improvement. A tick in the 'positives' column.

The unmistakable random thumps and booms of a soundcheck pull me downstairs. If I wanted, I could get there blindfolded. It's as familiar a route as that from bedroom to dinner table in my childhood home. Past the entrance desk, then 16 steps down, always taken two at a time. A 180-degree turn to the right, then six more steps, usually taken in one leap to suggest that I was someone of great importance and busyness. But, on landing, be sure not to smash into the ultra-stiff double doors at the bottom.

Immediately on the right would have been the small bar, invariably doing a roaring trade in room-temperature cans of attractively cheap Trent Bitter. Beyond that, cut into the back wall, was the equipment room, a pitch-black storage facility which also housed the DJ booth. To the left was the stage, an unremarkable construction whose only point of interest was the four-foot-wide pillar directly in front of it. While doing an important job – that of helping to prop the main university buildings up – the pillar nonetheless meant that the sightline of a band's lead singer was ludicrously compromised.

For old times' sake, I take the stairs as I would have done back in 1989. The first flight disappears in eight strides, before that pivot to the right and a leap to clear the second, shorter flight in one. But I'm not as fleet of foot as I was when I was 20. I'm carrying rather more ballast now. And someone's oiled those stiff double doors. My momentum sends me crashing straight through them and into the throes of the soundcheck. A number of heads turn – and not in a good way. There's a sea of scowls and disapproving glances from tour managers and roadies and all the other unspecified personnel making up Eliza Doolittle's entourage.

Even Eliza herself sends a glare my way from the stage. I bravely get on with doing what any self-respecting 21st-century citizen would do in such an awkward social situation. I skulk into a dark corner and pretend that I've just received a text message that requires urgent attention.

From this dark corner, I can see the light. It's bright, piercing. And it's close. Twenty yards away, at most, on the far wall. I stumble towards it, weaving around flight cases and tripping over cables. As I cross the hall, I notice that toilets have finally been installed down here. Previously punters had to climb three flights of stairs to go and relieve themselves. Or simply fill up the nearest empty plastic pint glass. Long-overdue toilet provision is unquestionably good news. This is progress. Another tick.

But the neon that's luring me across the room, moth to flame, is spelling out a word that's instantly souring the memory of my alter mater. A single, two-syllable word that will sink the heart and deaden the pulse of anyone emboldened by the snakebite-and-mosh-pit appeal of live music in its rawest, most elemental state. One single word that sits high on the far wall, rendered by a fluorescent tube fashioned into a jokey, let's-take-life-lightly font. One fucking word.

Cocktails

Let's get this straight from the start. As delicious and refreshing as they might be in certain tropical climes, cocktails do not belong at gigs in provincial British towns. They mean a smarmy Tom Cruise tossing his shaker all over the shop in a cocky manner that's never going to impress any woman with half a brain. Or they evoke an image of Wicksy behind the bar of The Dagmar in Albert Square, keeping those jacket sleeves up to the elbow as he fiddles with the graphic equaliser to get the most from his new Shakatak cassette. Cocktail culture is simply bad news. There's a reason why Phil Oakey rescued the cocktail waitress in *Don't You Want Me*, why he picked her out, shook her up and turned her into someone new.

Granted, there are the innately sophisticated cocktails – Martinis, Black Russians – that belong to a more classic era. But there are also those ordered by big-salary, small-dick nobheads who, giggling with uncontrollable adolescent excitement, request a Slow Comfortable Screw from the barmaid, to be swiftly followed by a Screaming Orgasm. Oh, save my aching sides.

Gig-goers should not be drinking these. Live music is served by the pint. Or in bottles or cans. Them's the rules. It's beer, it's cider. Or it's both together in the same glass, with a dash of Ribena. Now *there's* a cocktail.

The debacle doesn't end there. To the right of this cocktail bar – and its neon sign that is clearly *laughing* at me

– is an area that has something of the boudoir about it. Apparently, it's the VIP section, all pinks, golds and reds, chaises longues and chandeliers. The fuck?! Just what is this monstrosity doing here in what was this dungeon-dark, sticky-floored nirvana? Rather than keep itself as a larger version of The 100 Club, it's been turned into China Whites. Or at least one corner of it has.

Let's calm down. Why should I expect the place to be just as I left it – a freeze-frame of (what I believe to have been) better times? This is the next generation's turn. They're not trespassing on my patch. This is their playground now. But still I can't escape the feeling that my years were better times in which to be a music-loving Essex student. And I'm fairly sure that my recollections aren't tinted, that they've not been smoothed and amplified by the passing years. Indeed, to make sure I was coming here with reliable evidence to hand, on the way up to Colchester I took a detour via suburban south-east London to track down my old Ents pal Josh.

We hadn't been in contact for the best part of two decades but segued straight back to where we left off, when he disappeared to Italia '90 and I left on a jet plane to live in Minneapolis for a year. Trading war stories back and forth, it appeared that my recollections held pretty true (or, of course, it could be that Josh's have become equally tinted, smoothed and amplified).

There was the time that a certain lower-league rock band rolled up and, even before inspecting the dressing room or sniffing the freshly laundered towels, requested that someone score some good-quality recreational drugs for them. One of the Ents goths was able to satisfy this demand within a couple of minutes, quicker than any promoter had managed on the whole tour. We were so proud. Then there was the time Josh and I tried to get John Peel out of the shower. We were contractually obliged not to publicise that The House Of Love show – a secret warm-up gig for a week-long residency at the ICA – outside of Colchester, but wagered that Peel might be up for 'accidentally' breaking the embargo for us on air. Sadly, his pre-show cleansing routine took priority over a phone call from a couple of cheeky chancers.

One of the best stories comes from the night that headband-wearing Dire Straits frontman Mark Knopfler brought his spin-off group The Notting Hillbillies to our subterranean cave. The alleged and possibly apocryphal story goes that, on arrival, so cheesed off was Knopfler – a veteran of countless shows at top-ranking venues like the Hollywood Bowl – about playing such a comparative shithole with a big fat pillar right in his sightline, that he vented his anger on the nearest target. A tray of tea and coffee was sent sailing across a freshly scrubbed dance-floor by his left foot. Allegedly.

Those two hours spent reminiscing with Josh weren't the ideal preparation for me to play the objective observer this evening. How could the autumn term's one and only gig possibly compare to a few years of fondly recalled, sepia-toned memories? And when the doors open and the gig begins, I'm even further distanced from the whole affair. Just as I did among the metal kids at Bloodstock, I feel like a dad who, having dropped off his progeny, has hung around in an attempt to recapture the essence of his long-since-dissolved youth. Which is, of course, partially true. I just don't have any college-age kids to drop off. Not yet.

Taking a position near the back, I'm clearly from the wrong generation tonight. Eliza Doolittle herself wasn't even six months old when I first stepped into this hall back in 1988. And if policemen are getting younger, I can report that students seem to be too. And I certainly can't remember myself being so effervescent and so outrageously happy as tonight's audience. By the end of my own teenage years, cynicism had its hooks well and truly in me.

Having – of course – refused to give the cocktail bar my custom, I sip a rather decent Guinness and wait for Eliza and her band to take to the stage. The support DJ is playing something familiar, but I can only pick out the odd snatch over the hubbub of these loud, enthusiastic students.

"Woo-hoo! Woo-hoo!" I think it is. Yes, it definitely is. It's *Sympathy For The Devil*, The Rolling Stones' establishment-baiting belter from 1968. Goosebumps on my arms. Someone's pulling my chain. I'm sure we've all entertained the notion that we alone occupy the centre of the world and that everyone else is merely in a supporting role – that feeling so brilliantly realised by *The Truman Show*. I'm feeling it now.

Because if any one song, out of the millions committed to tape in the last half-century, is redolent of my Ents time here, it's *Sympathy For The Devil*. It was a totem track back in the Dancehall days, the third tune of a three-song mix that Ents stalwart Jez, a mature student from Halifax, would always play at the climax of every Friday night disco. If it was 1.45am, you could bet your bottom dollar that he'd put on Happy Mondays' floor-filling *Step On*, segue into The Stone Roses' *I Am The Resurrection* and then top things off with Mick and Keef's classic before the house lights came up. The students would then depart, "woo-hooing" their way back to the tower blocks.

I look around to see where the DJ is perched these days. I half-expect to see Jez, 20 years older and possibly greying at the temples, gurning back at me, playing the record having spotted his old associate in the crowd. But it won't be Jez. Josh told me earlier that he lives in Cornwall now. It's mere coincidence. Or, of course, it could be that it's a tune that's been played here almost every night for the last couple of decades, upholding a tradition started back in my day. I close my eyes and, as The Stones get well into the groove, imagine it's 1990 again. When I open them, that 'cocktails' sign rudely informs me that it's not.

The show itself passes off perfectly acceptably. Eliza is bubbly and buoyant and a decent-sized crowd is in – suggesting, of course, that they might fancy a little more of this new-fangled live music thing this term than has been planned. They're certainly very appreciative of Eliza's efforts, even if most seem to be hanging on for her recent Top 5 hit *Pack Up*. It certainly shows that they don't need a big-name DJ or a bubble party to have a fine old time. (Although far too many of them are gabbling away noisily with no regard for anyone else. Must be something in those cocktails.)

Gig over, I climb back up the stairs to ground level. Six steps up, 180-degree turn and a weary ascent up the remaining 16 steps. I stick my head outside. Back in the day, every Friday and Saturday night, a van would be parked up, hawking what were referred to across the campus as 'rat-burgers'. While there's no van any more, gig-goers now have a late-night snack-bar, offering a more exten-sive selection of after-midnight fare than most motorway services. I'm grateful for their generous opening hours and plump for a cheese-and-red-onion panini, another invention that had yet to reach Colchester in 1990. Alongside the venue's name-change and its new toilets, another tick goes in the book.

The floodlights of the Astroturf pitch have long been switched off as I head back up the hill to the car. I take a picture of Jane's old tower block to show her. It's not going to be a great photo – the silhouette of a tower block against a clear, pitch-black sky. It's my last souvenir. I suspect I'll never see the old place again.

Despite this very welcome and surprisingly good panini, I can't help but feel an overwhelming sense of dejection – and one not solely generated by the presence of that soul-deadening cocktail bar. From the paid assistance to the unyielding grasp of professionalism, a huge amount of Ents spirit has been lost. The age of charming amateurism seems heartbreakingly over, maybe finished forever. No more will young folk give up their Saturday afternoon for free to make an industrial quantity of sandwiches for The Icicle Works. Or spend an hour in the campus launderette, patiently spin-drying towels for the sweat-absorbing needs of the Tom Robinson Band.

Tonight I didn't see students joyously being involved in gig promotion just for the hell of it. We used to be so thrilled by the whole endeavour because we were often making it up as we went along. We learned from our mistakes. My time as part of the Ents crew became an apprenticeship where I developed the skills of thinking on my feet and of cajoling volunteers into action – attributes that have really come into their own when persuading sleepy, recalcitrant children to brush teeth/put shoes on/walk to school.

Now all the mistakes have been learned from. It's all about following time-practised procedures. Twenty years ago, we put in the legwork, promoting shows with paste and bucket, guillotine and photocopier. Student gigs are now almost exclusively promoted online – it's all about the length of your database and the number of your Facebook friends. Ents promotion now leaves little room for creativity and impulsiveness. What remains is a series of service jobs to be filled in students' unions up and down the land. They might as well be scooping fries at McDonalds.

I don't want that McDonalds experience. I want something home-cooked and un-homogenised. I want my live music experience to be put together by hand, by instinct. Not just by numbers.

On the drive back to the B&B, a dozen or so miles down the A12 towards London, I make a vow to find those kindly folk getting involved in live music just for the sake of getting involved, not for reasons of topping up their income or adding the experience to their CV. Although they seem to have disappeared from the students' union Ents community, these people, this rare species, must be out there. Endangered, perhaps, but hopefully not extinct.

11

IN THE NAME
OF LOVE

Destinations: Central London / the suburbs of Birmingham / the
   lonely hills of the North Yorks Moors
Occasions: Performances in run-down bandstands, erratically
   furnished upstairs rooms and bare-bones tin sheds
Miles travelled so far: 5,642
Chats with folk music royalty on a fire escape: 1
Flapjacks offered by fellow gig-goers: 2
Emergency stops for suicidal sheep: 3

The billows of blue cigar smoke rising towards the ceiling.
The Italian brogues kicked up onto the mahogany desk.
The mahogany desk the same colour as the leathery skin.
The big talk, the blather, the bullshit.

   We all retain a mental image of the music impresario.
More often than not, it's probably just taken from that
Kit-Kat TV ad from the mid-'80s, the one where a hopeful
young pop band has an audience with a dismissive record

company exec in his gold-disc-lined office. "You can't sing. You can't play. You look awful." A snap of a Kit-Kat finger. "You'll go a long way."

More modern times have updated the stereotype. It's now Simon Cowell, the pantomime villain with the high waistband, delivering those barely bothered put-downs while his mind is clearly elsewhere, probably busy calculating his hourly rate as he trots out those predictable slights and sneers.

Not all music impresarios look, or behave, like this. I suspect barely one per cent of them ever have, in fact. Certainly Ian and Thomas don't. And this pair are in no danger of getting rich any time soon either. They're not wearing Italian footwear, nor puffing on hand-rolled Habanos, but they don't seem to mind. For these twenty-something gig promoters are operating on a higher plane and aren't in the game for the money. They're simply doing it for the love of doing it.

As such, they resemble me and Josh 20-odd years back. Unlike me and Josh, though, their manor isn't a darkened, underground lair full of black-clad Sisters Of Mercy fans and Hawkwind apologists. Instead, they prefer the bracing feel of fresh air on their faces, the sound of light, bright indie-folk in their ears. Because Ian and Thomas run Bandstand Busking, a loose brigade of pals and associates who set aside their spare time to blow the cobwebs off the Victorian bandstands of London Town. Their objective is to revive the original use of these often crumbling structures, to reinstate the purpose for which they were built. Live music.

Ian and Thomas are in no danger of getting rich because not a single coin is changing hands today. They've set no price of admission. Nor do they pay their artists a penny. Instead, Bandstand Busking is an endeavour that puts on live music for live music's sake, each performance artfully shot and uploaded onto the collective's website. It's a mutually beneficial arrangement, a brilliantly conceived no-brainer. Punters get a free gig in a memorable setting. Performers are immortalised in a set of well-made films, effectively a showreel that touts their wares in the direction of potential new fans and record company executives (and also any promoters happy to exchange actual hard cash for their services).

And Ian, Thomas and their chums get a sense of deep satisfaction, one that's immediately evident from their ear-to-ear smiles and at-ease demeanours. A Bandstand Busking event is an occasion that suits all three parties – punter, performer, promoter. It's a win-win-win situation.

Today's 'busk' has been blessed by bright, white October sunshine. I'm among a 100-strong crowd that's descended on Northampton Square, somewhere in central London. I couldn't say precisely where. I don't know this part of the capital too well. I don't know it at all, if truth be told. It might be Finsbury, it might be Islington, it might be Clerkenwell. There are no tourist-friendly landmarks to guide me and this area's office buildings and apartment blocks all melt into each other. I'm a country boy used to a less cluttered landscape, to having a couple of miles of open countryside between each settlement. It's how us straw-chewing bumpkins can tell our Buckland Monachorums from our Nempnett Thrubwells.

I wouldn't call Northampton Square open countryside, but it's a patch of land that at least gives Londoners in this rather claustrophobic neighbourhood a little breathing space. Some city-dwellers might even, especially on such a gloriously golden day as this, declare this diminutive patch of green to be 'idyllic'. Certainly the cooing pigeons and mischievous squirrels add to the bucolic vibe.

We're all clustered around the bandstand in the centre of the square. Flanked on two sides by elegant late-Georgian townhouses and by the modern architecture of City University on the other two sides, this wooden structure is long overdue a lick or three of paint. But what it lacks in emulsion, it gains in emotion as a succession of unplugged acts earnestly take their turn at playing four songs apiece to the gathered assembly.

A peloton of pushbikes have been chained to the railings on the eastern side of the park, ridden here – if the neatly asymmetrical haircuts and diligently trimmed facial hair are anything to go by – from the graphic designer-heavy streets of Shoreditch and Hoxton. A handful of pushchairs and prams are parked up too, newborn babies given a genteel debut experience of live music. Their first gig. Many of the spectators join the performers in the shade of the bandstand; the remainder elect to keep their place in the sun. Passing shoppers surrender to their curiosity, setting their grocery bags down for five minutes to take in the sights and sounds. There's a sense of unhurriedness about the whole thing. It's like Eigg's Away Game – but without the woods and mountains and that temperamental body of water.

When things do get underway, its attractive ramshackleness is another reminder of the Away Game. The performers – largely folk-edged acts best suited to performances that, helpfully, require no electricity supply – tend to just drift into their songs, casually announcing the next number through the medium of chalk and blackboard. "People understand it's sort of ad hoc and slightly disorganised," whispers Thomas. "That's part of the charm."

Another part of the charm is watching these outfits at such close quarters that you could pretty much reach out and touch them. Accordingly, these bare-essential performances heap all eyes, and plenty of pressure, on the performers who are already under deep scrutiny thanks to the three video cameras trained on them. "It's a very different venue for the artists," Thomas confirms. "Here they've got people sitting at their feet. They've got to perform. There's no room for anything other than perfection."

This afternoon's four outfits all acquit themselves with aplomb, in particular Player Piano, the singer-songwriter from Indiana last encountered in a chronically hungover state in the marquee back on Eigg. This time he's in the company of two chums; collectively they sound like a less dysfunctional Violent Femmes. And in my book there's absolutely nothing wrong with sounding like the Violent Femmes, dysfunctional or not.

However, as full as this afternoon's bill of fare is (three other combos are playing – Tap Tap, The Lofty Heights and Stairs To Korea), this time yesterday it was a different state of affairs. A succession of withdrawals dictated that there was only one confirmed act lined up and ready to play. Cue a frenzy of phone calls and emails to plug the gaps. It's a spontaneous, make-it-up-as-you-go approach to live music that, as I've found out on my travels, is an increasingly endangered concept. And there are times when that's the best way to fly. There's nothing wrong with a little mild panic to take you out of your comfort zone, to make the heart pump a smidgeon faster. Thinking on your feet is a fine skill to possess. It's exactly why I've always preferred working for weekly magazines than for those whose glacier-slow schedules mean each issue only emerges every three months or so. We need adrenalin every once in a while.

With three replacement acts found at short notice, adrenalin is in short supply now, the tranquillity only once interrupted by a piercing ambulance siren that soon dissolves on the air. Despite the agreeable setting, not everyone's a fan of the Bandstand Busking concept. "There's a lady who lives in that house over there," announces Ian, nodding his head in the direction of the far corner of the square, "who doesn't like music being played in the bandstand." A snigger to mark the irony. "She caused some problems for us," continues Thomas, "so we have to jump through a certain number of hoops to get a licence. It's not very expensive – you just have to fill in the forms on the right date. But, if you were a parent wanting to put on a little gig for your children, it's just impossible."

Ian interjects. "We've been planning to write to Boris and ask him to make it easy for us. It's a good cultural thing, after all…"

Red tape seems to get everywhere. It pushes students' unions towards spirit-crushing professionalism and it means that a few friends can't get together to play some acoustic musical instruments in a public park. Nowadays, Bandstand Busking operate by the rules, no matter how heavy-handed and suffocating those regulations might appear to the rational observer. But Ian, Thomas and the gang didn't always play ball, such as when they had to jump over a padlocked fence to film a session in a band-stand in Golders Green. Then there was the time they recorded a performance by Of Montreal in Regent's Park. "We managed to convince the park keepers to give us a quarter of an hour," Thomas confides. "But we took a little longer. They said 'Alright, we'll walk the other way for another ten minutes…'"

The collective discovered that the capital's parks are home to no fewer than 35 bandstands – "the joy of Google Maps!" chuckles Ian. So began the reclamation of these Victorian structures from the possession of Special Brew-supping vagrants and bored teenagers.

I take my hat off to these guys. Well, I'd take my hat off if only it weren't now getting noticeably chilly as the sun begins its descent behind the square's tall buildings. The final chord of the afternoon has been struck and the last of the Hoxton-bound bikes have been unchained from the railings. The gathering has dispersed, a content crowd has departed. The neighbourhood's dog walkers are now retaking possession of this small park. A scruffy terrier seems particularly pleased to have found some sandwich crusts that an audience member has left on the grass as an offering to the local pigeons.

And I'm particularly pleased with what I've found here on this lazy, sunny afternoon – a procession of prom-ising acts, plus an altruistic, for-the-hell-of-it attitude that enriches the capital's cultural life. It's to the benefit of the greater good, rather than to the benefit of an individual's pockets, exactly as Greg, the lead singer of The Lofty Heights, told me earlier. "Promoters in London don't promote. They just let the bands do it. So I really like this vibe. You don't have to listen to a corporate jukebox and buy overpriced beer in some pub. Just put it on yourself. Do a guerrilla show."

If the young men and women behind Bandstand Busking are guerrillas, they're the politest, most well-meaning freedom fighters imaginable, enlisting acoustic musicians to their cause, ukuleles and video cameras their weapons. While the ad hoc nature of the operation might suggest slight similarities with the meet-in-a-motor-way-services-car-park-and-await-further-instructions nature of illegal raves during those innumerable summers of love in the late '80s, here there are no constabulary-evading tactics. Indeed, with the video gear now packed away, a couple of the team are making sure that any litter discarded by their audience has been safely deposited into the nearest bin.

Usually, the next job for a promoter would be to head off to the counting-house to tally up the takings. Here, though – in a week when the tickets for a Jay-Z show at Alexandra Palace were all snapped up in less time than it takes Usain Bolt to cover 200 metres – there's no financial reward for their endeavours. Quite the opposite, in fact. Each member of the collective actually chips in a modest amount of their own money to keep the show on the road. Or, rather, keep the show in the bandstand. "It's less than we'd pay if we all went to these bands' gigs," reasons Thomas, citing previous appearances from the likes of Ed Harcourt, Guillemots, First Aid Kit and Speech Debelle. "It's just a cheaper way of us seeing them."

And he's got his eyes on cheaper ways of seeing some genuine musical A-listers. "I want Björk on a bandstand! And the troupe of colourful people she'd bring with her. And, of course, if Thom Yorke popped down and said he'd like to do a little piano session, we wouldn't turn him away..."

※   ※   ※   ※   ※

There isn't a single interior designer alive, whether they had their own Channel 4 show or not, who would have been remotely impressed with the appearance of my gran's living room. It had, erm, character. There was nothing unified about either décor or furniture. Even to my young eyes, it was clear that the mustard-yellow rocking chair was no friend to the floral-print armchair and the burgundy carpet.

I feel like I'm back there – albeit on a much larger scale – here in the upstairs room of a large, rambling pub in the Birmingham suburb of Kings Heath. Arranged in neat rows are about 100 chairs of varying dimension and design. But, even if some of the seating has seen better upholstered days, a duff spring or well-worn seat cushion still provides more comfort than the moulded-plastic chairs favoured by village halls and community centres – those utilitarian brown ones that numb your bum in minutes flat. No, homely is what this room is. The heavy velvet curtains and mildly psychedelic purple carpet complete the look.

Welcome to the Red Lion Folk Club.

For its clientele, this upstairs room represents folk music heaven. Downstairs, dejected Aston Villa fans are drowning their sorrows after this afternoon's comprehensive defeat to Chelsea, seeking solace in the bottom of a pint glass, therapy through the occasional frustrated burst of swearing. Meanwhile, politely queuing on the impressive wooden staircase (which, I'm later informed, enjoys listed status), the folk club audience barely raises its conversation above a whisper. The cultural contrast couldn't be any starker this Saturday evening. Downstairs, the quick-changing vagaries of Premiership football. Upstairs, the granite-like permanence of the English folk tradition, as personified by tonight's performers, the husband-and-wife folk duo Martin Carthy and Norma Waterson.

Having run for nearly 40 years, the Red Lion Folk Club is currently in the care of another husband-and-wife duo, Della and Chris Hooke, aided and abetted by a team of ever-present volunteers. The club won the BBC Radio 2 Folk Award for Best Folk Club in 2006, a salute to the efforts put in by the whole Red Lion team, especially as it was voted for by the actual musicians on the folk circuit. And it's a team – like our old Ents crew – who give up their Saturday nights just for the love of it. It's quite a commitment from all concerned, as Della – a retired, and acclaimed, landscape historian in her other life – explains.

"Running it has quite a few ancillary demands. It takes a lot of time up and you've got to have some money behind you in case of problems. If you make a loss one night, it might be a long time before you can recoup it. And we've got a big house so we can put the performers up at weekends." Indeed, the life of a folk club organiser is not dissimilar to that of a B&B proprietor – cleaning the house, making beds, cooking soup. There's just the small matter of a gig right in the middle of things.

Then there's the stress of attracting big enough audiences to avoid underwriting the whole endeavour from your own savings. "It isn't easy to get it to a new audience,"

Della sighs. "Fifteen hundred people will turn up to Birmingham Town Hall, but they won't try a folk club where there's a far more intimate experience. Many will never have been to a folk club in their lives. They may have no idea what one is. They may have an image from the '60s or '70s when these clubs were smoky drinking places, but those days have totally gone. They'd find it very pleasant indeed. It's just getting them here in the first place.

"On the whole, our audience isn't young. It's 50-plus, I'd say. We do our best to get youngsters in, but they like to go somewhere they can talk. We are a pretty serious and silent venue. We're like a little theatre." Were anyone intent on offering a single whispered mid-set observation to the person next to them, I imagine that Della would make a pretty formidable peacekeeper, ssshhhing people from the sidelines with all the fervour of a militant librarian. Not that she needs to. Later on, the audience will, to a person, become completely transfixed by one of the complicated, multi-verse ballads that Martin Carthy specialises in, utterly absorbed by all the narrative's nuances.

For now, while the support act runs through its sound-check, I nab Martin for a quick chat. This is Martin Carthy, the English folkie whose music was undeniably a major influence on the young Bob Dylan and the even younger Paul Simon in the folk clubs of early-'60s London. Indeed, Simon famously later failed to acknowledge Carthy's adaptation of the traditional song *Scarborough Fair* when Simon & Garfunkel released their decidedly more commercially successful version. I suspect that Paul Simon's income for just that one particular hit is a significantly larger amount than Martin Carthy, this stalwart of the modest-paying folk circuit, has earned in his entire career.

As someone absorbed by his records in my teens, I'm thrilled to be getting a ten-minute audience with the man himself, now well into his pensionable years but still wearing a pair of silver hoops in his ears. It's a balmy evening, so we retire outside, squeezing onto the Red Lion's fire escape. While the traffic hums past below, he explains how indebted the folk musicians of this country are to bands of volunteers like Della's.

"Entirely! Without them, the whole thing would not work. This network of volunteers is the most extraordinary thing about the folk scene. It's entirely anarchic and apparently arbitrary, but it's worked ever since it started. There are very few clubs that don't work. And there are very few chiselers. There's one or two inevitably, but they are known and fingered and despised!

"We could not have survived without these people. They decided to open a folk club because they love it, they absolutely love this music. They have survived almost completely without outside funding. They haven't got any money, they do all the publicity, they book the room, they set out the chairs, they put the artist up, give them breakfast in the morning and take them to the station. These are good people. They're your number one fans. And if they don't like you, they let you know. I promise!"

Brian and Rose are two crucial members of the Red Lion team whose respective associations with the club stretch back to the '70s. Brian, a burly fifty-something with a soft Brummie accent, first came here as a punter, before "gradually weaseling my way in as a general dogsbody". He's been operating the sound desk for the last ten years. His commitment to the cause is shown by the fact that he's only missed one Saturday night show in all that time. And he can be excused that single blip in an otherwise immaculate record – he was otherwise engaged taking part in a 24-hour snooker marathon for Children in Need. Even when the club shuts up shop for the summer, Brian can be found volunteering at folk festivals.

The thrill has never left him. "If we've had a good gig, at the end of the night I'm as up as the artists. And if I do cock something up – which is most unlikely but it does happen! – I'll be thinking about it all week."

Rose, too, was originally a punter, taking her place on one of those well-used chairs. "Then, before you know where you are, you're selling raffle tickets and you've become part of the scenery. Back in the '70s, lots of women wouldn't have dreamed of going into a pub on their own. But you could go to a folk club and quickly feel part and parcel of the place."

Rose – who, with her glasses, neat silver hair and calm demeanour, is the double of an old primary schoolteacher of mine – looks after the artist hospitality and is happy to give me a guided tour of the dressing room. It's not a lengthy tour; she calls it the "dressing cupboard". It's effectively a couple of chairs and a table full of neatly arranged light refreshments – tea bags, mugs, bottles of water. Simple sustenance, but always appreciated by the visiting artists with their eye on a few home comforts. Indeed, when the musician Jon Boden, de facto leader of folk big band Bellowhead among other allegiances, was supplied with Jaffa Cakes one Saturday night, he passed on his thanks "to the biscuit committee", prompting Rose to get a T-shirt made with the legend 'biscuit committee' on the back. I've never gone a bundle on the idea of committees, but I'd turn up for every meeting of that particular one. Where do I sign?

Just like backstage at Cardiff International Arena, the dressing room walls are lined with pictures of artists who've previously stepped on stage here. "They're all dead!" laughs Norma Waterson from her position, sat in the corner of the room. If they are all dead, no-one's showing much respect for the deceased. Moustaches, beards and glasses have been scribbled onto faces in biro by those who've used the "dressing cupboard" over the years. Many of these venerable folk artists now resemble either one of those Marx brothers – Groucho or Karl.

Live music's fortunes may wax and wane, but every Saturday night, Della and her team are here. Rain or shine, full house or half-empty room. Doing it as they always have done. And it's a scene that's replicated right across the country. Freeze-frame the action on any given night and, in the upstairs rooms of pubs from Fishguard to Frinton, similar loose bands of volunteers have surrendered their time in the service of folk music. They've done so quite possibly to the detriment of their love lives – and almost certainly to the detriment of *The X Factor*'s viewing figures.

And also across the country, audiences – grateful for the organisers' dedication to the cause – sit in close quarters to their folk heroes, nursing halves of Guinness and packets of McCoys, careful not to crunch too loudly during a particularly intense ballad about a grisly episode of sororicide.

I've been to one or two folk clubs – plus a handful of folk festivals – before, mainly in my twenties, directed there by the records of The Waterboys or the Oyster

Band or Christy Moore. But they felt like a closed shop, alienating. Places where, if an audience member didn't understand a reference to Pete Seeger or have an intimate knowledge of the life of the renowned song collector Cecil Sharp, they'd feel an outsider, held at arm's length. The cliché about folk clubs has always been that they're populated by real-ale-supping, Fair Isle jumper-wearing insular types. It's now become a cliché to dismiss the original cliché, but some truth still lies there. Every cliché has its foundation in reality.

Unless the night's main act was a young thrusting folk act packed with attractive twenty-somethings brandishing accordions and fiddles (bands like Wigan's Tansads or Boiled In Lead, a favourite act of mine from my time in Minneapolis), truth be told I found these clubs staid and a bit worthy. Rather than crucibles of wild abandon, they tended to be full of solo folkies earnestly tackling traditional material that, quite honestly, would have been better off had it been abandoned a century or two ago. No-one seemed to be having too much *fun*.

If I were at a Boiled In Lead gig, I'd have wanted to hurl myself around the room in an unsightly manner, especially when they took flight on one of their numbers that fused together tunes from Ireland and Eastern Europe. The seating plan of a folk club puts paid to that. Back then, I wanted to consume live music while having my ribs pressed hard against a stage barrier or sliding across the dancefloor on a sea of spilt lager. Not perched on a chair, legs crossed, nodding sagely.

So what's changed for the folk club experience to now appeal to me, here as I take my pleasingly comfy seat? Has my attention span improved to the extent that I can better appreciate subtlety and nuance, that I don't need a rousing chorus of massed instruments to keep my interest? Or is it simply that my ageing limbs no longer thank me for being hurled around a room, that they'd prefer a nice sit-down instead?

I'm rather thankful that I no longer need a bone-rattling stack of speakers, an elaborate light show and a pea-souper cloud of dry ice to enhance a performance. Good job, too. Folk club gigs are rarely slickly choreographed shows. Tonight's is certainly no squeakily polished performance. Norma frequently takes out her hankie to wipe her nose, while also occasionally forgetting the lyrics of songs. She has three goes at *Ain't No Sweet Man Worth The Salt Of My Tears*. But the audience aren't looking for slickness or choreography. In the folk world, it's not about artifice and stagecraft. It's about the songs – and the honesty and integrity they're performed with.

But I note they're not so keen on audience participation. When Norma invites them to join her on *My Flower, My Companion And Me*, only a gentle murmur rolls across the rows as they timidly join in on the chorus. I can sympathise with this reluctance. The price of admission has been paid to hear the professionals up there on the stage, not the wrong-key notes of the chap in the next chair.

This is part of a bigger issue – the proximity, nay overlap, between artist and audience. I'm conflicted on the matter. On the one hand, I can appreciate the ego-free, all-in-it-together atmosphere. As Loudon Wainwright proclaims in *Harry's Wall*, his song about fame and the encroachment of fandom: "They're just like you and me!" I was certainly very much taken by those bandstand performances, and those in the ceilidh hall on Eigg, for that matter, where your proximity to the musicians meant you could almost smell what they had for lunch on their breath.

On the other hand, if you've paid an unearthly amount of cash to see your heroes, you expect an unearthly presence and an unearthly performance in return. Something of a spectacle from someone who doesn't look like he or she has just stepped out of the audience, someone looking just as shambling, scruffy and unwashed as yourself. As the young (that is, younger than me) folk musician Jim Moray once opined to me, "I want to be taken to another place when I go to see somebody. All that 'I'm just like you' presentation undermines the songs which might be magical and mysterious and extraordinary. Presenting them in an ordinary way feels like a travesty."

I may well favour the latter view, where the division is upheld, where at least the illusion of star quality prospers. Don't meet your heroes and all that. There's plenty of hypocrisy here, mind. I am, after all, the man who once sneaked through the stage door at Portsmouth Guildhall to thrust his hand into that of Michael Stipe. I'm the same man who once harangued Stipe's off-duty bandmate Mike Mills in a Minneapolis nightclub with an endless barrage of asinine questions about the album REM were at the time recording at Prince's studio Paisley Park. And I'm also the man who compromised the gentlemen's agreement between fan and artist by doggedly collecting the autographs of the lesser members of Prefab Sprout with all the diligence of the most committed stalker.

Whichever approach is the correct one, tonight the divide between performer and punter is erased. During the interval, the more forward audience members approach Norma to pose for a photograph or ask Martin about the significance of particular lyrics. Perhaps they're requesting a pithy overview of his adaptation of the traditional ballad *The Famous Flower Of Serving-Men* – all 30-plus verses. Even if their backstage accommodation were more generous, you get the sense that Norma and Martin would still spend the interval out among the people. Their people.

Those choosing to keep their distance instead form a single queue at the bar, patiently waiting for their turn to place their order with the lone barmaid. Just as I liked the crush of stage barrier on skin when I was younger, so too did I enjoy the cut and thrust of trying to get a drink in a busy venue – all sharpened elbows and trod-on toes. Like battling pensioners at a village hall jumble sale – only less violent. Indeed, right at this moment, unholy jostling is doubtless breaking out in the overpriced bars of venues across the land. These days I appreciate the undeniable civility of an orderly queue.

At the evening's end, by which time the Aston Villa fans downstairs have departed for home and a drunken re-examination of the afternoon's events on *Match of the Day*, Norma and Martin are down from the stage again, back among us for as long as we want them to be, excellent ambassadors for the downright decency of the folk community. There's still time for the raffle, though – that folk club fixture and a financial necessity for such a shoe-string endeavour. There are two prizes up for grabs – a pair of tickets for next Saturday's show ("It's Beck Sian. She's Kate Bush's cousin!") and a box of chocolates. I'm crossing my fingers for the chocolates and the sugar rush I need to stay awake on the southbound M5.

It's not to be. The box of Milk Tray is swiftly claimed by a woman in the second row. The gig tickets will be soon, too – but not before we get another example of the charming, gloriously un-slick ways of a folk club.

"It's yellow!" Della calls out. "99!" Silence. No-one claims it. She turns the raffle ticket the other way up. "Or is it 66…?"

❀ ❀ ❀ ❀ ❀

The North York Moors are a strange place to try if you're looking for the heart of Saturday night. I'm a long way from home. I'm a long way from anywhere. Yet here I am, having made a left turn when I reached the middle of nowhere before travelling a few more miles past the back of beyond. (Sadly, though, as lengthy as my journey is, I reach my final destination without having to pass through – and therefore enjoy a photo opportunity in – the excellently named hamlet of Fryup.)

It was an assault course to get up onto the moors, the Honda testing its credentials for the RAC Rally of Great Britain by roaring over spine-realigning cattle grids and swerving around gormless sheep that have little regard for the Highway Code. These are roads untouched by the Night Bus. And I'm breathing air that has never been scented by the unmistakable post-gig odour of a kebab shop. Toto, we're not in Camden any more.

And by God, it's dark. Proper dark. Can't-see-your-fingers-in-front-of-your-face-until-they're-poking-you-in-the-eye dark. Well, save for some glowing lights just down the hill that come welcomingly into view, that is. These are the lights of the local village hall, burning orange through its windows, looking like a rectangular Halloween pumpkin. 'Village hall', though, is something of a misnomer. The village we're in – Low Mill in the valley of Farndale – isn't strictly a village. It barely qualifies as a hamlet. I can count the number of its houses on one hand.

And, as village halls go, this is surely one of the UK's tiniest. It's little more than a corrugated tin shed, its battleship-grey external walls enlivened by the racing-green front door and red tin roof. You'd think that just the lightest breeze would send it scattering in dozens of pieces across the surrounding moorland. But this minuscule building has shown plenty of resilience over the years. Built back in the 1920s as the headquarters of the local silver band (essentially the same as a brass band, only with its members playing silver-lacquered instruments), it's known simply as The Band Room. And, in recent years, it's returned to its original purpose. Just like those London bandstands, its stage now bursts with music. On one Saturday night a month, at least.

The music that resonates around its wood-panelled walls is no longer made by the area's sheep farmers and iron-ore miners taking out their instruments of an evening for another run through a brisk Sousa march or Rodrigo's more stately *Concierto de Aranjuez*, the stirring tune memorably referred to as "Orange Juice" by the Grimley Colliery Band in the film *Brassed Off*.

The Band Room's performers these days are almost exclusively found among the folk/country constituency, their instruments plucked and strummed rather than polished and blown. While plenty of homegrown names have graced the stage (Cerys Matthews, Kate Rusby, our friends Norma Waterson and Martin Carthy), the venue has made its reputation by putting on shows by numerous touring American artists, among them Willy Mason, Howe Gelb, Laura Veirs and Allison Moorer, the singer otherwise known as the seventh Mrs Steve Earle. This tin shed clearly makes an impression on these itinerants. The Chicago-based alt-country combo The Handsome Family proclaimed it to be "the greatest small venue on Earth". They're right. It's a terrific room – bare-bones basic, but homely and deeply atmospheric. The antithesis of the arena, and therefore the perfect place to be engaged and enveloped by live performance. I feel like I've come home.

You might expect me to be reporting that, once inside, The Band Room takes on Tardis-like attributes, boasting a roomy interior that accommodates its 100-capacity crowd with a surprising level of comfort. But it doesn't. While we might not be invading each other's personal space in quite the manner of sardined commuters on the Victoria Line, we will be watching tonight's performance while getting to know our fellow gig-goers pretty intimately.

There's barely enough room in here to swing the overfed cat that has to be ejected from the stage before tonight's main act comes on. Perhaps the moggy has got plump thanks to titbits offered by the audiences here over the years. Before the music starts, the air is full of the sound of popping Tupperware lids as homemade flapjacks are released and scoffed. Our feline friend will later take care of any dropped crumbs. And, being as how the venue's modest capacity would need to be halved were they to install a bar, liquid refreshment comes on a purely bring-your-own basis. Clink-clink go the bottles of ale being pulled from numerous bags-for-life.

Another American is playing tonight – the singer-song-writer Jesca Hoop. Most of the attention directed towards

Jesca's career thus far has made much mention of her past job, that of being nanny to Tom Waits' kids back home in California. This serves to ignore her music, of which I'm a big fan; music which that particular gruff-voiced past employer has perfectly described as "like going swimming in a lake at night".

Just as those labyrinthine Martin Carthy ballads totally absorbed the Red Lion audience, so too are Jesca's songs mesmerising everyone here in this tin hut. The music's slightly Gothic spookiness is perfect for a location straight out of *Wuthering Heights*. And, without the slightest whisper of background chatter, everyone who's made the trek up to this windy, windy moor is being sucked into her spell. The twinkling fairy lights framing the small stage just add to the feeling we've been transported into another world.

"I really do love these tight-knit shows," Jesca tells me afterwards, once the spell has been broken. "You can almost exchange eye-to-eye contact with everyone in the room. And I enjoy the freedom you can have with conversation. You can reach everyone directly. If the room is too big, you're talking to no-one. You can't tell who you're talking to.

"Everyone's there for just one purpose. There are no distractions. It would be seen as completely obscene were they to talk. And, of course, there's no mobile phone reception!"

That overfed cat, no doubt on the scrounge for a scrap or two from the rider, has come 'backstage' – that is, the small back room where, in decades past, the silver band presumably set up the hot-water urn for a brew halfway through rehearsal. Despite the distractingly loud purring,

Jesca continues on her theme, applauding those behind low-capacity venues like The Band Room who put shows on for spiritual, rather than financial, gain. "People want to contribute to the cultural wealth of their community. One thing is certain. If you come to a small place in a small town, you're going to get a dose of the town. And you're going to get people who really want to be there. The larger the venue, the more diluted the audience becomes."

Nigel, the leader of the bunch of friends who put on these semi-regular Band Room shows, knows just how special this shack is. And while you might think he'd be cap-in-hand grateful for whatever touring act was prepared to make the trip up to deepest, darkest North Yorkshire, it's actually the opposite. In a show of bravado that I really rather admire, Nigel sets the bar nice and high.

"Shows are few and sometimes far between," declares his manifesto on the venue's website, "while we wait for our principal targets to become available – so we try to make every show count. There are no ordinary acts, no perfunctory gigs, no fillers. We have no spring or autumn schedule to cobble together. Life's too short. Before we book anyone, we always ask the same question: are they good enough to play here?"

And if an act does pass the audition, they will also find their set-list being ever-so-slightly dictated by the Band Room team. Every performer is requested to slip a Bob Dylan cover into their set. Tonight Jesca opts for a shimmering reading of *Tangled Up In Blue* which earns purrs of approval from Nigel and his pals.

They're clearly big Dylan fans to a man. This is emphasised later when Nigel reveals what would be his ultimate booking for The Band Room – Robert Allen Zimmerman himself. Even though outwardly I'm nodding and smiling politely, Nigel can tell that, under the surface, I'm doubting the feasibility of his pipe dream. He shoots me a long look that tells me he's deadly serious. The maths has been done. He knows of 100 people who would willingly pay £1,000 to have such an up-close-and-personal audience with His Bobness, convincingly arguing that Dylan would need his head examined were he to turn down £100,000 for an evening's work where he wouldn't have to share the proceeds with a roadie-heavy entourage.

I couldn't stretch to justifying – let alone getting my hands on – a grand for a single night's entertainment. But if I didn't live 280 gear-jamming miles south-west of The Band Room, I'd be here like a shot every time its battered green doors opened for more modest business. It's just that special a place. I get chatting to one regular who never misses a gig here. And it's not as if he himself lives nearby. Graeme's home is in Morpeth, 20-odd miles north of Newcastle. It's a five-hour round trip for him for each show. It's an impressive commitment, but still less than half the mileage I'd cover every time I aimed the Honda towards the M1.

This is one of several preposterously long journeys I've made for a single music event in recent months – I'm thinking of the snow-bound schlep to Durham for Half Man Half Biscuit and the car/plane/bus/train/boat marathon that was getting to Eigg. But the drive to North Yorkshire and back seems to have worked some magic.

All those miles represent serious thinking time, hours and hours of quiet contemplation – as long as you switch off those sanity-sapping radio phone-ins. No word of a lie, but on the way up (and I'm ashamed to say it was during a programme on BBC Radio Bristol, a station for which I used to be a regular contributor), I was astounded by the question of the day with its deeply held Reithian values: 'What's the best biscuit?'

Even though I know the answer to that particular conundrum (Janet in Mangotsfield was wide of the mark when she suggested the fruit shortcake; it is, of course, the never-disappointing bourbon), I've got weightier issues on my mind as I head back south. At some point on the way home – quite possibly in the Nottingham area – I have an epiphany. My thinking becomes crystallised. The fog has lifted.

If I'm still a little uneasy with the ways of the 21st-century gig-goer, if I can't stop myself getting even mildly annoyed by the background chatter and the through-the-nose drink prices and the what-the-hell-is-that-for booking fees, plenty of what I've seen and heard on these thousands of miles *has* relit my fire, has helped me to become smitten with live music once again. But I'm still not head-over-heels in love. For that to happen, I need to be doing more than observing from the sidelines. Too much punter, not enough protagonist.

I should follow the example of Nigel in the wilds of Low Mill, of Della and her team upstairs in the Red Lion, of Ian and Thomas in whatever central London bandstand they're currently occupying.

I should just do it myself.

12

BRINGING IT ALL BACK HOME

Destination: The Louisiana, Bristol
Occasion: Devon Sproule/The Pictish Trail double bill
Miles travelled by journey's end: 6,002
Posters put up: 120
Flyers handed out: 650
Money made: zilch

I'm blinking back into sunlight, emerging out of the darkness.

Metaphorically, at least. In a more literal sense, I'm blinking into the bright stage lights that render everything and everyone beyond them a vague, indistinguishable dark mass. But they're there. I know this from the cheers that greet my words when I tell this vague, indistinguishable dark mass (otherwise identified as a collection of the most refined music fans the city of Bristol can muster) exactly who are going to be entertaining them this evening.

After 6,000 miles of gear-jamming my way along those blue lines of the road atlas, I'm back on home turf in the West Country. Specifically, I'm on stage in the upstairs room at The Louisiana, for many years one of the leading venues in Bristol and the city's token tribute to the architecture of New Orleans' French Quarter. Every town has their equivalent of The Louisiana, their own compact and bijou nightspot played by many acts on their way to international stardom. In Glasgow, it's the terrifically named King Tut's Wah Wah Hut, the place where Alan McGee first clapped eyes on Oasis. In Oxford, it was always The Jericho Tavern. York has Fibbers, Southampton has The Joiners. And, down the road in Bath, it's my old stomping ground of Moles.

Why am I on stage? Have I discovered a hitherto untapped proficiency on the tambourine? Am I going public with a bunch of soul-searching songs I've been secretly penning for years? Thankfully for the ears of this near-full house, the answer is "no" on both scores. Instead, tripping over the amps on the way to the mic, tonight Matthew, I'm going to be... the Promoter.

There are many people I've met over the last few months who can take the blame for this. Barry from ATP taking arch, cool bands into what could have been holiday-camp hell. Bloodstock Paul putting on a big-scale, but defiantly non-corporate, festival. The Fence Collective's wobbly but charming knees-up in the Inner Hebrides. The Band Room's near-cocky insistence, despite its geographical isolation, to only book bands it feels are worthy of the location. The just-do-it spirit of the bandstand brigade. They all had big dreams and crazy schemes, and they all made them flesh. And now each one has inspired me to get off my lazy arse, to turn my own pipe dreams into reality, could-haves into have-dones.

And I'm rather satisfied with the double-headliner show I've dreamed up: our old friend from Eigg, Johnny 'Pictish Trail' Lynch, and the Ontario-born, Virginia-raised singer-songwriter Devon Sproule, as seen on *Later... With Jools Holland* and big stages like those of the Queen Elizabeth Hall and Shepherd's Bush Empire. Both are acquaintances (I've known Devon since she was the subject of the first feature I wrote for *The Guardian* years ago) and, despite their respective homes being far, far from here, both happen to be within an hour's striking distance of Bristol on the same day. Kismet or coincidence, the pair's dual proximity is too good an opportunity to resist.

Here at The Louisiana, I'm standing on the very spot where many future stars would have stood as they nervously tried to paper over any musical deficiencies with brag and bluster. Younger, possibly spottier versions of The White Stripes, Fleet Foxes, Super Furry Animals, Amy Winehouse and The Strokes have all trod these modest boards. Muse are celebrated/ridiculed (delete as appropriate, according to taste) for their ridiculously histrionic stadium shows, the polar antithesis to the basic frills offered by this cramped room above a Bristol boozer. But play it they have.

Like those young wannabes, I'm also up on this stage nervously papering over any deficiencies with brag and bluster. Not the host with the most. More like the host with a modicum. Standing right in front of me is the familiar figure of Big Jeff. Big Jeff is something of a local hero, a gentle giant who's down the front at all the gigs that matter in Bristol, instantly recognisable by both his mane of frizzy blond hair and his frequent willingness to watch gigs bare-chested. He's such a hero among the local gig-going fraternity that a documentary has even been made about him. His presence in the front row suggests that tonight's gig is the hottest ticket in town. The stamp of approval.

As a double bill, tonight's star turns complement each other well. Devon's a slight, little bird who, having grown up on a hippie commune, retains all the free spirit that you'd assume such an upbringing would bestow upon her. Johnny, by contrast, is a plaid-shirt-wearing, bearded bear of a man whom I describe to one potential ticket-buyer as possessing "the voice of an angel and the sartorial elegance of a lumberjack". If Devon and Johnny comple-ment each other physically, I reckon – as the two halves of a double bill – they'll musically dove-tail neatly together. They've enough shared artistic sensibilities for fans of one to appreciate the other.

I've had a soft spot for double bills ever since that Pop Will Eat Itself/Derek B show during my freshers' week. But they're a bugger to make financial sense of, espe-cially if you're an independent promoter with the cost of venue hire to factor into the equation. As I'm effectively forking out for two headliners (rather than paying a far more reasonable single headliner fee, plus a low-paid/free support act), the money is tight. As tight as the proverbial gnat's chuff, in fact. I've always been one to put artistic concerns ahead of economics and tonight I've done so in quite ludicrous fashion. Sir Alan/Lord Sugar would have a fit if he saw my calculations and would doubtless reduce me to a quivering wreck were I to present these figures in

The Apprentice's boardroom. Tonight, I will only slip into profit should the venue pretty much sell out – my break-even point is set at the room being precisely 97.8% full. Harvey Goldsmith is not quaking in his size 10s.

Acknowledging my lack of hard-nosed business sense, I've been finding as many ways to keep costs low as possible. For starters, Devon and Johnny are staying at our house (respectively occupying hastily purchased sofa bed and hastily repaired inflatable mattress), meaning that I can secure their services for a little less than normal as they won't be coughing up for the services of the nearest Travelodge.

To maximise my chances of at least breaking even, I've also called in a few favours. Like asking my graphic designer chum Alun – to whom I've given a lift home after five-a-side every Monday night for the last eight years – to design the poster for free.

I've also gone begging to my buddies in the local press corps. Time was when I'd be guaranteed some gushing editorial in the pages of the Bristol listings mag *Venue* (for which, remarkably, I was once employed as editor). This coverage would usually be enough to evaporate any concerns I might have over numbers. Such was the trust the readers put in its cultural recommendations that tickets would just fly out of the door.

But, three months ago, just as it was celebrating its 30th birthday, *Venue* ceased to exist as a publication, at least one that got well thumbed, folded, ripped and left your fingers an inky mess. Its presence is now merely online, where, of course, there are a great many other sources of information available at a click of a mouse. As a result, *Venue*'s loyal, easily defined and ever-discerning readership is now more diffuse, no doubt using a variety of means to organise their social life. Or they're simply not going out any more. I need to find these people.

Despite *Venue*'s untimely demise, the local printed media that still do exist are kind to me and the gig gets gushing write-ups in three or four publications. But, as blessed as I am with the press coverage, I can't ignore the online world. Since I last promoted a gig nearly a decade ago, Facebook and Twitter have revolutionised the way that word gets out, so I put some thought towards a digital campaign. Although I'm conversant with the ways of Twitter, its 140-character simplicity within even my own limited grasp, I need a crash course in Facebook from my pal Paul. At the end of this crammer session, I'm none the wiser, but Paul has set up a dedicated page for the show and assures me that everyone in the Bristol area who needs to know about this gig will very, very soon know about this gig.

But it's tough and the handful of other independent promoters I know around Bristol all report sluggish sales for their gigs, with very few shows guaranteed to put even a modest wad of cash in their pockets. My gig might still be a good few weeks away, but taking a hefty financial hit isn't an option. I can't leave it to chance. There's no insurance policy.

So I launch a concerted promotional push, this time using some good old-fashioned tools which feel good in my hands: posters and flyers, Blu-Tack and sticky tape. I ratchet up the number of gigs I'm willing to stand outside of in the rain in the vain hope that, when flyers for my show are thrust into their collective mitts, the departing audience will instantly rejoice. Or, more importantly, immediately phone up for tickets. All too often, and rather selfishly, I feel, they seem more preoccupied with catching the last bus home than with ensuring my return to live music promotion is a successful one.

Despite only being a half-hour drive away from Bristol, I end up putting in nearly as many miles on poster/flyer duties as I did driving to Colchester and back. And sometimes the wait outside a venue can be lengthy. At one particular gig, the headline act plays well beyond the venue's curfew. When I politely point out to its staff that he really should have stopped playing by now so that I can hand out these flyers and skulk off home, I'm – equally politely – informed that the curfew only applies to amplified music. The bugger's merely unplugged his instrument and is now playing an acoustic set which, in theory, could last all night. I'm just going to have to wait. In the rain.

There are other occasions when I don't need to wait at all. Like at a Nanci Griffith concert at the Colston Hall in the city centre. I'm excited by the prospect of several hundred of the Texan's acolytes getting all unnecessary at the prospect of Devon, another country-tinged troubadour (and one currently resident in Nanci's home town of Austin, no less), coming to their town. By 10pm I've taken up my position just beyond the Colston Hall's automatic exit doors, a wad of flyers in either pocket and the collar of my coat upturned against the chilly evening breeze. Ten past comes and goes. So does 20 past. Strangely, not a soul has left early, no-one happy to miss the encore's big numbers in exchange for a swift exit from the multistorey car park across the road.

I step through the automatic doors. The foyer is curiously quiet. On the other side, there's a table where the merchandise man is laying out his wares. A welcome sign of life. The only thing is that he's not laying out his wares. The closer I get, the smaller the piles of T-shirts and CDs are getting. And the fuller the boxes are becoming.

Me: What time's she off?
Him: Off? She's all done.
Me: Is she doing encores yet?
Him [slower]: No, she's all done. She's finished. She's played already.

It takes me a while to compute this information, for my end-of-the-day brain to make sense of it.

Me: But I've been here since ten.
Him: 9.50 she finished. She's probably back on the bus by now. Everyone's gone home. The place is empty.

9.50? Nine? Fifty?! Who the hell finishes that early? T-Shirt Man reminds me who. Nanci Griffith, that's who.

But early-to-bed country singers are the least of my problems. Every other day during the three weeks before the gig, I head to Bristol with a roll of posters on the passenger seat, seeking out prime, A3-sized gaps on walls and windows. In one particular pedestrian subway, I must have put up a dozen posters. Every time I go there, the poster I put up a couple of days before (on a legitimate poster site, I must add) has invariably, predictably disappeared. So up goes another, the ritual repeated.

And then there's the sandwich shop where, despite its walls being covered in posters for upcoming gigs, mine are also being removed or pasted over. It's extremely frustrating. The unwritten rule of the gig promoter – that a poster stays in position until the event has happened – is being broken left, right and centre. Or, as the more hopeful side of my brain suggests, they're being half-inched by fans of either Devon Sproule or The Pictish Trail as pre-gig souvenirs.

My poster patrols are relentless. I go everywhere – record shops and bars and newsagent's and cafés and bookshops and clothes emporia and indoor markets and pubs and flower stalls and venues and ticket shops and office block lifts and friends' front windows... I even leave my car parked up for a week in a residential south Bristol street (one that has what the marketeers would describe as good 'footfall'), each and every window plastered with posters.

Despite the sluggish sales causing me a little panic, I'm kind of relieved that promoting still needs to be more than just an armchair pursuit, that it can't simply be completely taken care of by someone in front of a computer screen. Hands still need to get dirty. And, I have to admit, I am loving getting out and about, making a small contribution to the cultural make-up of this city.

I even tried to involve the kids. I thought Finn would love nothing more than to pound the wet, chilly streets of Bristol for hours on end as we doggedly searched for available poster sites. I even said he could be in charge of the Blu-Tack. No dice. It appears that he'd much rather spend the time in his warm, dry bedroom, listening to his *Mr Majeika* audiobook while being supplied with another plate of cream crackers and cheese. The youth of today...

Despite Finn's reticence, this gig is a team effort. Jane's welcomed the pair into our house, making the upstairs office into a cosy room for Devon to stay in and baking an enormous lemon drizzle cake that proves a huge hit with two touring musicians grateful for some home cooking. Ned's surrendered his pirate-themed bedroom for a couple of nights to Johnny and his multiple on-tour rucksacks, while Finn's spent a full two hours fashioning a guitar out of Lego, should an additional instrument be required by either musician.

But still – unlike up in The Band Room, upstairs at the Red Lion or in those bandstands – I've not got even a modest team of volunteers willing to sacrifice their own free time to help stave off my impending bankruptcy. Instead, for my own little gig, I'm pretty much everyone and everything.

When it comes to feeding Devon and Johnny, I've heeded the three-course lesson of Vicky, Elbow's chef – that a band marches on its stomach – and, before we leave home for the venue, I rustle up some food that stands up pretty well in comparison to Vicky's menu. I'm also the B&B proprietor, welcoming musicians – and their debauched rock'n'roll ways – into our home. Thankfully, neither bedroom is equipped with a portable TV that could be spectacularly discarded out of the window. Nor is there a swimming pool into which could be driven a Rolls-Royce. Or even an elderly Honda Civic Estate. No, the most debauched that the pair's stay gets is when Johnny launches a 2am assault on whatever cheese he can find in the fridge.

Of course, it's not just about bed and board. I've also got a variety of roles at the venue. I can now call myself a roadie again, although carrying just a pair of guitars the 20 yards from car to venue does not a lengthy load-in make. Then, once all that heavy lifting's done, I bury myself in the dressing room, putting the pre-mixed gin and tonics on ice and setting out enough sandwiches and salted snacks to feed a regiment. And then I'm on emcee duties, my spotlit gabble just about fit for purpose. I didn't forget their names, at least. That's a distinct improvement on my wedding speech.

And I'm also the support act. Rather, the CD I've just handed Duncan the soundman is the support act. Naturally I was always going to call upon my skill-set here – the boy who fast-forwarded through his teenage years by imposing his music taste on others through the medium of compilation tapes was never going to pass up the opportunity of doing likewise now he's in his forties. There's a captive, near-capacity audience to indoctrinate, after all. I've put plenty of music from my travels around this isle on the CD, partly to suit what I think the evening's mood will be and partly to provide a few moments of contemplation for me as I approach journey's end. There's no Modern Romance or Meshuggah admittedly, but there are top-quality tunes from the likes of King Creosote and Jesca Hoop and Sweet Baboo and Avi Buffalo and Dr John...

Sadly, though, the artistic balance and unerring good taste contained within the CD's 20-odd tracks is lost come showtime. You can't hear a note of any of them over the PA, such is the level of happy chat from an expectant room of Devon Sproule/Pictish Trail fans. But I don't mind that one bit. Better that than having every track hollowly echoing around a sparsely occupied room.

After my initial introduction, Johnny takes the stage and takes control. As someone who once tried his hand at stand-up comedy before becoming a professional musician, he's a curious mix of heartbreaking balladry and hilarious between-song banter. The crowd are on-side from the off, fuelling the bonhomie with some good-natured heckles. Even when he delivers a couple of decidedly off-colour gags, they go down a storm, thanks to his easy Caledonian charm. This is no spotless, silent arts centre gig, after all.

That said, it's largely pin-drop silent during Devon's set, her delivery very precise, her beautifully descriptive lyrics demanding close attention and appreciation. Despite the pair each doing an hour-long set, the evening is flying by with all the relentless charge of a speeding express train. After weeks and weeks of effort, I just wish everything was happening in slow motion.

But I'm delighted that both performers are going down a storm and allow myself to enjoy the moment. Gazing around the almost-full room, I muse on how, if the original thought hadn't slipped into my head, we would all be sat at home watching *The Great British Bake-Off* instead. Jane's standing next to me near the back of the room. A smile and a squeeze of my arm. I reckon she's having the same thought too.

After Devon's set – and with ten minutes left until the venue's immoveable 11pm curfew, a restriction in place because of The Louisiana's proximity to some expensive harbourside apartments – she calls Johnny back up on stage. There they each sing one of their own songs, accompanied by the other. On Devon's *If I Can Do This* and Johnny's *All I Own*, it feels like they've been performing together for years. I might have lost a few quid tonight, falling just short of that target attendance of 97.8%, but those last ten minutes of stage time will become a price-less memory.

I had advance notice that the pair of them playing together would sound rather special. Earlier this afternoon, they set themselves up in our front room to run through these two songs. The boys came home from school and, still in their uniforms, sat at Devon and Johnny's feet, faces full of wonder, a concert in their own front room. It appears that they've inherited my fascination for live performance.

An impression has certainly been made. Ned digs out his toy musical instruments and he and Devon are swiftly engaged in what can only be described as a 'jam'. Never slow to come forward, he appoints himself musical director and calls the shots. *Twinkle Twinkle Little Star* gets several run-throughs, mainly because it's the only song his four-year-old fingers can play on his little keyboard. And play it he does, note-perfect. Tomorrow, suitably inspired, he will announce that he's formed a band. They're called Zig. I've certainly heard worse band names. Dumpy's Rusty Nuts, for starters.

Jam session over, Ned and Devon disappear upstairs like a pair of pop pixies to compare favourite YouTube music clips on her laptop. Later, Finn shows that he may well have inherited my music journalist genes too as he cross-examines her about one of her songs – *It's Good To Get Out Of The House*. Just why is it good to get out of the house? And Devon's answer – something along the lines of it being beneficial to get out into the world, to interact with people, to experience this little spinning planet in the brief time we have here – has perplexed this young lad who, given the option, would spend every waking hour in his bedroom with his box of Lego. He'd already missed out on the character-building experience that is going on poster patrol.

I've not been a promoter since I became a father (helping to organise pirate-themed kids' birthday parties just doesn't count). I know this because the morning after the last gig I put on, Jane revealed that she was pregnant with Finn. Today – the day I'm returning to the promoting fray – is the very day that Ned starts school. A clear circle is being completed, those early years of parenthood neatly, albeit unintentionally, parenthesised by my life as a promoter. Its own little subordinate clause.

I appreciate I might be parping a little too loudly on my own trumpet, but this first gig back has been rather special. Certainly downstairs in the main bar afterwards, as Devon and Johnny sign and sell a few CDs, those audience members enjoying one last drink for the road seem all aglow. Several punters come up to shake my hand and pass on their thanks. Among them is Big Jeff. He's beaming with satisfaction. Profit margin be damned. That smile, from a man with, I guess, a good few thousand gigs under his belt, is all the validation I need.

In the morning, I drive Johnny back into Bristol and drop him off at Temple Meads. He's got a long journey back to Eigg. Indeed, after missing a train connection at Glasgow and having to undertake a 150-mile taxi journey (as well as a choppy voyage across *that* body of water), he won't cross the threshold of his static caravan until nearly 36 hours later.

My own journey home should take 30 minutes. But I'm stretching it out. Just as on that walk back from school all those months and miles ago, the one where I came up with the original idea of hitting the highway. I'm out for a ridiculously long time. Despite dropping Johnny off at the station during the morning rush hour, I don't get home before lunchtime. Another plan is being hatched.

I'm very much taking the scenic route, down lanes that lead I know not where. At almost every T-junction, there are posters of an imminent Wurzels show due to take place among the hay bales of a nearby farm. It's an evening's entertainment that both saddens my heart and strengthens my resolve. I want to feed the locals – my neighbours – more nutritious cultural fare. Putting on a gig in a major metropolitan area is one thing. But I need to bring it all back even closer to home, to contribute to, as Jesca Hoop called it, the cultural wealth of my community. This morning's zigzagging up hill and down dale is a round-the-houses search for my own tin shack, my own Band Room. It must be here somewhere.

Between stops to peek through the windows of village halls and to recce potentially convertible farm outbuildings, I mull over where I've been and what I've done over these past months. Bottle-dodging at Bloodstock. That Michael Eavis prank. Emergency treatment in a festival field hospital. Rides in golf buggies. Gladioli shopping for Morrissey impersonators. Swerving around sheep on windswept moors. Chronic sea-sickness. And an awful lot of falafel, pies and chips. It's been a fine old time. And, against all odds, the car's held out too.

But mostly I'm thinking about last night. All this time and all these miles, I've been looking for the heart of

Saturday night. And, at approximately 8.30pm yesterday evening, in front of a microphone in an upstairs function room, I found it. And it was only Tuesday.

Time has moved on since I first headed out all those long, long months ago. The boys are a little bit older, a little bit taller. A few baby teeth have now disappeared. And Spider-Man has been replaced by Stars Wars as the object of their affections (although, I'm delighted to report, Half Man Half Biscuit appear to remain a constant in their lives).

Some changes have taken place within me, too. I've made peace with live music – she's back in my life. My blood still simmers over inexplicably high booking fees and overly talkative audiences and prime-ministerial walkabouts, but it calms when I think about all the lovely people I've met, their inspiring passion and commitment, the adventures I've had and the great performances I've seen. There's a spirit of independence that still runs strong through the live music world. It may now run even stronger as a response to the domination of faceless corporations and ruthless sponsors trying to claim all the territory for themselves.

I'm one of those independents. The gig might have cost me a little cash, but it's a drop in the ocean when compared to the therapy I would otherwise have had to fork out for. Last night – and, indeed, this whole trip, all 6,000 miles of it – has been a peripatetic counselling session, guiding me towards making peace with changed realities, with new responsibilities and with the slipping-by of the years.

Thanks to all those live music experiences – the least spiritually demoralising ones, that is – my groove has returned. And even though I don't find that ideal rural venue this morning, I'll be out searching again tomorrow, just as soon as I've got the kids dressed, made them breakfast, checked their homework, packed their lunch boxes and deposited them at the school gates.

I'm still the devoted father, but I'm also the returning promoter, my identity renewed. I'm now more than simply Finn and Ned's dad waiting for the home-time bell. There's ambition in my heart again, fire in my gun.

Mr Gig is back.

ACKNOWLEDGEMENTS

Huge thanks to everyone quoted in the text (too many to list by name, I'm afraid), both for their time and for patiently tolerating my ill-conceived questions and half-baked theories about live music.

For their unfailing ability to get me beyond the velvet rope, salutes are raised towards Alan Bearman, Sarah Boden, Nigel Burnham, Geoff Davies, Conal Dodds, Caroline Hunt, Lewis 'Loudhailer' Jamieson, Sam Jones, Jon Lawrence, Judy Lipsey, Ken Lower, Jessica McMillan, Sarah Pearson, Sarah Pickles, Tom Piper (twice), Adam Sagir, John Shearlaw and Charlotte Vikstrom.

For commissioning me to write for them between these various sorties along the lost highways of Britain, my mortgage payments are indebted to Mark Ellen, Kate Mossman and David Hepworth at much-missed *The Word*; Michael Hann at *The Guardian*; Adrienne Connors at *Sunday Times Culture*; Andrew Harrison, Chris Catchpole and Matt Mason at *Q*; and Rob Attar, Liz Barrett, Fergus Collins, Spencer Mizen, Dave Musgrove and Joe Pontin from the company formerly known as BBC Magazines.

For their encouragement, guidance or specific favours (or a combination of all three), hearty McCartney-esque thumbs-ups go out to Robin Askew, Rob Banino, David Barker, Sheryl Baxter, Andrew Collins, Jon Cooper, Tom Cox, James Fearnley, Luke Fitzmaurice, Eamonn Forde, Johnny

Green, Rich Guy, Jojo Harper, Alun Harris, Paula Henderson, Dave Higgitt, Mark Hodkinson, Jim Irvin, Bex Jones, Steve Lamacq, Janice Long, Johnny Lynch, Stuart Maconie, Paul McGuinness, James Medd, Jim Moray, Julian Owen, Lucy Porter, David Quantick, Pat Reid, Angela Rivers, Jude Rogers, Mig Schillace, Josh Smaller, Devon Sproule, Graeme Thomson, Rob Williams, Pat Williamson, Gordon Wise and James Witts.

For that initial cup of tea and for everything else since, I'd like to thank the team at Short Books, especially Aurea Carpenter, Roz Hutchison, Paul Bougourd and David Isaacs, my future rock-star editor. I'm also hugely grateful for the sanity-protecting calmness of my wise and resilient agent Susan Smith.

Most of all, though, I have to thank Jane for her love, support, bottomless patience and spot-on suggestions to improve the manuscript. And, of course, for covering the gaping holes in my domestic duties while I was hanging out with an endless stream of rock stars (or, more likely, while I was sat alone in a motorway service station, eating a lukewarm panini at 2am with a couple of hours of driving still ahead of me).

You've been a lovely audience. Have a safe journey home. Until the next time, thank you. G'night!

Nige Tassell is a music journalist whose writing has appeared in *The Word*, *Q*, *The Guardian*, *The Sunday Times* and *New Statesman* among others. He lives in the hill country of Somerset with his wife and two primary-school-age Half Man Half Biscuit fans. *Mr Gig* is his first book.